A POINT OF VIEW

Lisa Jardine

Drawings by Nick Wadley

preface

Published by Preface 2008

2 4 6 8 10 9 7 5 3 1

Copyright © Lisa Jardine 2008

Drawings copyright © Nick Wadley 2008

Lisa Jardine has asserted her right under the Copyright, Designs
and Patents Act 1988 to be identified as the author of this work

Nick Wadley has asserted his right under the Copyright, Designs
and Patents Act 1988 to be identified as the illustrator of this work

First published in Great Britain in 2008 by
Preface Publishing
Random House, 20 Vauxhall Bridge Road,
London SW1V 2SA

Address for companies within The Random House Group Limited
can be found at:
www.randomhouse.co.uk/offices.htm

The Random House Group Limited Reg. No. 954009

www.rbooks.co.uk
www.prefacepublishing.co.uk

A CIP catalogue record for this book is available from the British Library

ISBN 9781848090194

Papers used by Random House are natural,
recyclable products made from wood grown in sustainable forests.
The manufacturing processes conform to the environmental
regulations of the country of origin

Typeset by Palimpsest Book Production Limited, Grangemouth, Stirlingshire

Printed in the UK by Clays Ltd, St Ives plc

Introduction

It is a rare privilege to be allowed ten minutes of uninterrupted broadcasting time on BBC Radio 4 on a subject of one's choice, over a period of ten or more weeks on a regular basis, and certainly not an opportunity to be taken lightly. When the ten minutes in question are at ten to 9 on a Sunday morning, and the broadcasting slot the one for so many years occupied by Alistair Cook's *Letter from America*, that privilege becomes a responsibility.

Nevertheless, I can honestly say that writing and delivering my broadcasts for the *A Point of View* slot which has replaced *Letter from America* has given me an enormous amount of genuine pleasure. In part at least this has been because of the wonderfully active participation of the faithful and gratifyingly numerous Radio 4 listeners.

When I embarked on my first series in spring 2006, I

imagined such talks would be a rather lonely affair since, unlike the lectures and seminars I have become so accustomed to delivering throughout my career as a University Professor, there is no way of judging the response of the invisible listeners. Nor, I believed, would I be able to benefit from the kind of feedback one always gets from one's audience at the end of a platform talk of any kind.

As it turned out, I could not have been more wrong. From my very first broadcast, letters and emails from listeners supplied me with fascinating observations and additional pieces of relevant information. These enormously enriched my experience writing and delivering the talks and, indeed, put me on my mettle. No imprecision of meaning or expression gets past the regular BBC Radio 4 listeners!

The set of letters and emails I found most personally rewarding came in response to two talks in particular, one in each of the two series contained in this book. The first was my piece about J. R. R. Tolkien and the Battle of the Somme. The second was the one I wrote immediately upon hearing the news that the *Cutty Sark* was ablaze at Greenwich.

Many listeners wrote to say how moved they were to discover that Tolkien had been in the British trenches at the Battle of the Somme, and had lost close personal friends there. A septuagenarian clergyman wrote to tell me that he had heard from Tolkien's son that the Dark Riders in *The Lord of the Rings* recalled a nightmare moment in Tolkien's own experiences of war.

My talk about the shocking accident which destroyed the *Cutty Sark* while the ship was being restored and renovated produced a flood of correspondence, some of it about the ship itself, but a great deal more about the old philosophical conundrum, with which I ended, known as 'Is this my grandfather's axe?': My father replaced the blade of the axe, and I replace its handle. So is it still my grandfather's axe? How much replacement of the fabric of the *Cutty Sark* would it take, I asked, before it ceased to be the same ship?

Listeners who had reflected on this puzzle for the first time came up with some engaging reflections. Since 98% of the atoms that make up the human body at this moment will have been replaced 3 to 6 months from now, several asked, will I then be the same person? I was delighted to think of Radio 4 listeners engaging in such philosophical musings as they went about their daily business, and felt that I might have contributed in some small way to encouraging intellectual debate.

Indeed, the purpose of my *A Point of View* broadcasts will continue to be just that: using events in the historical past to stimulate discussion about important contemporary issues. Each week, as I develop my original idea, I imagine the conversation I might have with a listener I have chanced to encounter (such encounters do indeed take place). What would she or he have to say in response to my argument? How can I leave the question I am asking open enough to encourage my listener (and now, my reader) to take the thought further, and provide their own answers.

I aim to provoke, but I also hope to give pleasure, and even sometimes amusement. Perhaps, indeed, I might occasionally manage to make my listener or reader smile.

One

IN APRIL 2006 I MADE A LUCKY DISCOVERY IN THE PEPYS
LIBRARY IN CAMBRIDGE, WHICH ALLOWED ME TO CORRECT THE
HISTORICAL RECORD. IT CONCERNED A PIECE OF DOCUMENTARY
EVIDENCE REPEATEDLY USED TO PROVE THAT A DUTCH SCIENTIST
HAD BEEN THE FIRST TO INVENT A CLOCK ACCURATE ENOUGH
TO DETERMINE THE PRECISE POSITION OF A SHIP ON THE OPEN
SEA. MY DISCOVERY PROMPTED ME TO REFLECT ON THE GENERAL
ISSUE OF SCIENTIFIC PRECISION, AND WHETHER SCIENCE EVER
CLAIMS TO DISCOVER ABSOLUTE TRUTH.

Sometimes if you are lucky as an historian, you find a bit of
evidence which illuminates a big idea. That happened to me
in the Pepys Library at Magdalene College, Cambridge. The
thought uppermost in my mind as I worked my way through
the manuscript materials I had gone there to see, was how

odd it is that non-scientists think of science as being concerned with certainties and absolute truth. Because in fact the contrary is the case: scientists are on the whole quite tentative about their results. They simply try to arrive at the best fit between the experimental findings so far and a general principle.

The manuscript I found in the Pepys Library was a ship's journal kept by a seventeenth-century English sea-captain, who had offered to give space on his ship for some state-of-the-art scientific equipment – two new pendulum clocks – on a voyage to the east coast of Africa and back. The job he agreed to undertake for the recently founded Royal Society was to test the clocks at regular intervals on his journey, to see if they kept accurate time in spite of being tossed up and down and generally shaken about at sea. I'll come back to how he got on in a moment.

Science, as I say, is not doctrinaire. Strongly held religious beliefs, however, are. In the same week that I was transcribing seventeenth-century handwritten records in Cambridge, John Mackay from Queensland, Australia, an extreme advocate of Creationism, was touring halls and chapels in the UK attacking Darwin's theory that the human race has evolved gradually from the apes over millions of years. Mackay is one of those who maintains that Genesis is literally true, that the earth is a mere 6000 years old, and that the exquisite organisation of nature is clear proof that God's hand lies behind all of creation. During his visit Mackay had hoped to debate the matter with leading British scientists. If evolution is 'true', the Creationist challenges, step up and prove it.

There is something rather attractive about absolute beliefs.

Most of us find the idea of certainty comforting: 'The sun will rise tomorrow'. Uncertainty, on the other hand, is much more unsettling.

One of the reasons why we find it difficult to make up our minds about climate change and global warming is that the data are so complicated. Glaciers are melting, holes are detected in the ozone layer, emission of greenhouse gases is rising, yet we have just gone through an unusually cold winter, spring is unseasonably late arriving and it seems to have been raining continuously for months – it is hard to get alarmed. Scientists tell us that analysis of the current experimental data suggests that over the next 90 years sea-levels are likely to rise well over 10 centimetres – which means that entire coastlines will disappear. But even a passionate advocate of the prospect of impending ecological disaster like the Prime Minister's scientific advisor Sir David King, cannot, as a scientist, go so far as to say, 'It will be so. That is the absolute truth of the matter.' Instead TV and the newspapers offer us extensive coverage of the ecological scientists' warnings and doom-laden predictions, and we have to make up our own minds.

It is a basic requirement of scientific method that a tentative explanation has to be tested against observation of the natural world. From the very beginning scientists have been suspicious whenever the data fit the hoped-for results too closely.

Which brings me back to my clock-testing sea-captain, and the ship's journal I was reading recently in Cambridge. I was looking for documents relating to attempts by the seventeenth-century Dutch scientist Christiaan Huygens to develop a pendulum clock which would enable mariners to find their longitude at sea (their precise east-west position on the surface of the globe).

In 1664, shortly after the first proper scientific research institute, the Royal Society, had been established in London, its President, who was an admirer of Huygens's work, offered to organise a series of sea-trials to be conducted by the English navy, using two of his pioneering clocks. Precise locating of a ship's position at sea was absolutely crucial for naval warfare, as well as for ensuring that they could navigate clear of rocks and shoals. Captain Robert Holmes, commander in charge of the Navy ship the *Jersey*, agreed to take the clocks along with him on a six-month voyage down the east coast of Africa. He would keep the clocks wound and in working order, take regular measurements, make the necessary complex calculations, and supply detailed documentation in support of his findings.

When he got back to London in 1665 Holmes presented his report to an expectant Royal Society. The clocks had performed spectacularly well. Indeed, he declared, they had actually saved the expedition from disaster. On the return journey, Holmes had been obliged to sail several hundred nautical miles westwards in order to pick up a favourable wind. Having done so, the *Jersey* and the three ships accompanying her sailed several hundred more miles northeastwards. At which point, the four captains found that water was running worryingly low on board. Holmes's three fellow-captains produced three competing sets of calculations of their current position based on traditional reckoning, but all agreed that they were dangerously far from any potential source of water. Not so, declared Holmes. According to his calculations – based on the pendulum clocks – they were a mere 90 miles west of the island of Fuego, one of the Cape Verde islands. He persuaded the party to set their course due east – whereupon, the very next day, around noon, they indeed made landfall on Fuego, exactly as predicted.

London was abuzz with excitement. The Fellows of the Royal Society were elated, and immediately rushed Holmes's account of how the pendulum clocks had saved the day into print. Orders began to be placed for the revolutionary new timekeepers.

But the inventor himself, Christiaan Huygens, was not so sure. And his reason for being more cautious than his London colleagues was precisely the fact that the clocks had proved so astonishingly accurate:

'I have to confess,' he wrote to the Royal Society, 'that I had not expected such a spectacular result from these clocks.'

And he went on: 'I beg you to tell me if the said Captain seems a sincere man whom one can absolutely trust. For it must be said that I am amazed that the clocks were sufficiently accurate to allow him by their means to locate such a tiny island.'

Well, Robert Holmes was not 'a sincere man'. In fact, he was a rather notorious rogue. History remembers him as the man whose thuggish and piratical behaviour towards the Dutch merchants along the Guinea coast in the 1660s directly caused the second Anglo-Dutch war.

So the Royal Society asked an official from the Navy Board, Samuel Pepys – the same Pepys who wrote the diary – to check the evidence Holmes had provided against the day-by-day entries in his ship's journal. Pepys went off somewhat reluctantly to dine with Holmes – he confessed that he was rather afraid of him. Well, that was the journal I went to look at in Cambridge. Lo and behold! it turns out that Holmes had greatly exaggerated. The pendulum clocks had proved no more accurate for calculating longitude than conventional methods; the ships had been well and truly lost; the mariners had been extremely lucky to make landfall on the island of Saint Vincent several days after they turned back eastwards, just before their water entirely ran out.

Holmes thought that by tampering with his evidence he would please the scientists at the Royal Society. Instead, the too-precise nature of the match between his data and the results they wanted alerted them to the fact that his testimony was unreliable. And Huygens was right to be sceptical. His pendulum clocks never did prove accurate enough at sea to solve the problem of finding longitude.

A scrupulous scientist like Huygens would rather be disappointed than accept dubious evidence to provide pat confirmation of a pet theory.

And that continues to be true in all areas of scientific investigation today. Which is why no scientist would take up the Creationist Mackay's challenge to 'prove' the truth of Darwin's theory of evolution in a public debate. They knew they could not present a strongly held view based on a body of supporting evidence with the absolute certainty of a revealed truth. The most today's Royal Society was prepared to say was that a belief that all species on Earth have always existed in their present form, and that the Earth was formed in 4000 BC was 'not consistent with the evidence from geology, astronomy and physics'.

And that is probably not enough to satisfy ordinary thoughtful citizens without a scientific training, because most of us want certainty. It makes us feel safe. We're on the side of the seventeenth-century ship's captain, believing the experiments ought to prove the scientific theory once and for all.

Unfortunately, where arguments about the ecology are concerned, time is not on our side. We cannot afford ourselves the luxury of waiting for evidence which clinches the theory. We are going to have to learn how to participate in debates which are not about certainties. We are going to have to get used to asking ourselves questions in the form: Is this theory consistent with the evidence currently available? A public understanding of science has never been more important.

Personally, I am absolutely certain that a literal belief in a unique and perfect moment of Creation, presided over by an omniscient Deity, is no help in making important decisions concerning the here-and-now – like whether we should sacrifice our right to cut-price air-travel around the globe in order significantly to cut carbon emissions. At this crossroads in our planet's history, faith is no foundation for understanding slow and incremental climatic change, and the increasing likelihood that the human race faces an imperfect ecological future.

Two

ONE OF THE PLEASURES OF TEACHING GRADUATE STUDENTS IS
ACCOMPANYING THEM TO CONFERENCES ABROAD, SO THAT THEY
CAN GAIN EXPERIENCE IN INTERACTING WITH SCHOLARS
TRAINED IN DIFFERENT ACADEMIC MILIEUX. IN SPRING 2006 WE
ATTENDED A CONFERENCE AT THE UNIVERSITY OF GHENT. OUR
TRIP, JUST BEFORE 'EUROPE DAY', LED ME TO REFLECT ON HOW
ALIKE THE HABITS AND ATTITUDES OF BRITISH TWENTY-SOME-
THINGS AND THOSE OF OTHER EUROPEAN NATIONS NOW ARE,
WITH ONE IMPORTANT DIFFERENCE.

On a train from Brussels to Ghent in Belgium, the ticket
inspector asked me in English where I was getting off.

'Ghent [Chent]' I answered, with what I hoped was an
impeccable Flemish accent, anxious to indicate that I was
willing to make an effort, and showing off, I suppose, for the

benefit of the young colleagues travelling to the Anglo-Dutch history conference with me. He responded with a torrent of incomprehensible Flemish.

'Sorry', I responded hastily, in some embarrassment, 'I mean 'Ghent' [Guent]'. He lapsed immediately into flawless English. Which was just as well, since the information he was trying to give to us was that in order to leave the train at Ghent station, it was necessary for us to be travelling in the front four carriages of the train.

As we were to discover during our three-day stay, the Belgians and the Dutch move effortlessly between Dutch (or Flemish as the Belgians would prefer), French and English. They are competent German-speakers, and not averse to trying their hand at Italian and Spanish. Their linguistic confidence is palpable. It literally shows on the faces of those who serve you in shops and restaurants, or take your tickets on trains. In the Low Countries you are greeted fearlessly, with cheerful attention and direct eye-contact. In whatever language you speak to them, they are pretty sure they will be able to understand and respond appropriately.

To my twenty-something-year-old British travelling-companions this felt truly European. They expressed delight, not only at the shared, effortless means of communication, but also at the extraordinary similarities in interests and outlook between themselves and the young Dutch and Belgian historians at the conference. They all shopped at cheap-and-cheerful clothing stores like Hennes and Zara; they spent their leisure time engaged in the same pursuits: downloading music, going to the movies . . . and, it soon turned out as we got to know our fellow-conference delegates better, digging their allotments. They shared tastes in food and holiday destinations.

In the week leading up to Europe Day [9 May] this all sounds wonderfully optimistic. The founding charter of the European Union extolled the virtues of a multilingual community, of shared values and mutual respect among the member states. The new, ill-fated draft constitution, voted into oblivion last year (though recently revived as a new treaty), first by the French and then by the Dutch themselves, reaffirmed those commitments.

But while the rest of Europe embraces the variety of European languages, Britain seems bent on becoming ever-more determinedly monolingual. A recent survey for the European Commission revealed that two out of three Britons are unable to speak a language other than English. The number of students studying A-level French has dropped by two-thirds over the past ten years.

Britons believe that there is really no need for them to learn any other European language, when in the end everyone aspires to speak theirs. It is true that in mainland Europe – particularly in the north-west – linguistic flexibility is encouraged and celebrated. But where speakers of several languages are gathered together (as indeed at our conference), they will almost certainly end up speaking English.

So does it matter that the British appear to have decided that they need no second European language? Personally, I think it does. I am myself of fairly recent immigrant stock; my grandparents arrived here from Poland and Latvia as economic migrants in the 1910s. As children, both my parents spoke languages other than English at home. Both grew up to speak flawless English themselves. The story my father used to tell us was that as a recent arrival from Poland, aged 12, he took a bus from his home to the Whitechapel Library (sadly closed in 2005), and there borrowed two books: Frederick Marryat's 1850s adventure classics, *Masterman Ready* and *Midshipman Easy*. We used to tease him that Captain Marryat's nineteenth-century nautical prose had helped form my father's elegantly precise and slightly mannered way of speaking English.

My sisters and I were raised in a home in which only English was spoken, but my parents insisted that we acquire a second language too. They were convinced that learning an unfamiliar language makes one conscious of the mechanics of language-speaking, how language works as the bridge between us and those around us. With a second language a speaker becomes aware of the way the words they use shape their capacity to think; the way choices of words and modes of expression nuance our feelings and enhance our imagination. I find I share that belief.

Of course, significant numbers of those living in Britain today do speak more than one language. The children of recent immigrants speak one language at home and another at school just as my parents did. Where they spoke Polish or Yiddish, these children speak Bengali or Hindi. At Westminster City School in inner-city London, where my own son went to school and I was for many years the Chair of Governors, almost half [49 per cent] of the 750 boys speak English as what OFSTED calls an 'additional language'. Are these, then, potentially the flexible, outward looking members of our community who will be able to keep pace with the multilingual inhabitants of mainland Europe?

Mind you, although the average British teenager seems confident that English will enable them to get by anywhere, the EU administration is equally clear that no one language ought to be allowed to dominate. The compilers of European Union documentation still refuse to acknowledge the fact that English has become Europe's *lingua franca*, insisting that the languages of all the member states weigh equally. To the obvious question, 'Why not adopt a single language for business?', posed on an official website, the answer given is categorical: There is no obvious language to choose. The EU language with the largest number of native speakers is German; the European languages with the largest number of native speakers worldwide are Spanish and Portuguese; French is one of the official languages of three Member States (France, Belgium and Luxembourg).

As for English: 'Although it is the most widely known language, recent surveys show that fewer than half the EU population have any usable knowledge of it.' Wishful thinking, I'm afraid. For ease of communication among the enlarged membership, for everyday business and exchange of information, English will inevitably be used.

This is not the first time that Europe has embraced a *lingua franca*. At the beginning of the sixteenth century, Latin was the language of choice for educated Europeans, who reserved their national vernaculars for commerce and the domestic sphere. The great linguist, theologian, author and educator Erasmus of Rotterdam – a favourite Renaissance figure of mine – presided over a pan-European educational system designed to instil good, elegant Latin into all citizens. In class-room textbooks and scholarly editions he argued that the language of ancient Rome contained within it the seeds of universal human values and an international ethic of compassion and tolerance. Erasmus's textbook, *On Copious Speaking and Writing*, which went into dozens of editions, taught the student how to say 'thank you for your letter' in 150 different, equally elegant ways. By mastering Latin, Erasmus maintained, anyone could become a European.

But around 1515 Erasmus began to identify himself, in the prefaces and introductions to his works, as a Dutchman – as someone whose ideas and values were rooted in the northern Netherlands. And he did so because he had begun to realise that it is not enough to identify with the shared values of Europe as a whole. Each individual still needed a sense of belonging to a smaller group, with whose customs and way of life they could identify. We cannot be sure what changed Erasmus's mind, but it marked the beginning of the rise of the European vernaculars, the emergence of the modern nation state, and the demise of Latin.

Watching the easy mingling of the young British, Belgian and Dutch at the conference in Ghent it was clear to me that they are all now confidently European in their habits and outlook. So perhaps I have reluctantly to concede that it may not be necessary for the British, who have the good fortune to speak the European *lingua franca* as their mother tongue, to be made to learn a second language. They can do all right without it, and, after all, they can learn any specified language later, as the need arises.

But if that is the case, then the pressure on English as our mother tongue becomes intense. Unlike our Belgian and Dutch neighbours, it is the only language we have in which to learn to understand ourselves and others. If (as Erasmus thought) our emotional bearings are rooted locally, in the language of the place we call 'home', then we are going to have to turn our attention fully and energetically towards English as the source and historical origin of understanding for the British Isles. In its rich literature and history, in the nuanced subtleties of its meaning, must lie our own peculiar sense of belonging. For us, English is far more than the twenty-first century European *lingua franca*. It is the bedrock upon which our sense of what it is to be British is built.

Three

IN THE SAME WEEK IN 2006 IN WHICH ARSENAL PLAYED ITS LAST GAME AT ITS ARCHITECTURALLY ICONIC HIGHBURY STADIUM, ENGLISH HERITAGE LAUNCHED AN APPEAL TO THE PUBLIC TO HELP SAVE THOUSANDS OF PARISH CHURCHES WHOSE FABRIC WAS THREATENED BY LACK OF FUNDS TO MAKE GOOD THEIR DETERIORATION. I WONDERED WHETHER 'CHANGE OF USE' MIGHT HELP SAVE CHURCH BUILDINGS WHICH WOULD OTHERWISE FACE DEMOLITION.

Arsenal Football Club has played its last game at its Highbury Stadium. Next season they move to their new Emirates Stadium a short walk away. On the day before the final match, I joined the thousands wandering around Highbury, paying homage. Dads clutched small children dressed in Arsenal strip by the hand, as they gazed intently up at the façade of the great East Stand. There was an eerie respectful hush, broken only by the clicking of many cameras. The iconic building was the object of an almost reverential attention – filled to overflowing with memories, the bricks and mortar in the process of becoming history.

In the press, former players recalled how amazed they had been by the 1930s state-of-the art facilities: the high ceilings in the bathrooms, the under-heated floors. They remembered having been bowled over by its scale. 'I'll never forget my first sight of Highbury,' Arsenal goalkeeper Bob Wilson reminisced. 'I remember coming down this tiny street opposite the main stand and thinking: "That's unbelievable." I was in awe. I have always said Highbury is a Cathedral, not a football ground.'

Something about the sheer extravagance and scale of a building like Highbury fills the onlooker with wonder. We are dwarfed by its grandeur. In its red and white, stylised splendour, it is a striking reminder of our own smallness. It draws us in, towards the greater group which congregates there and succeeds in filling the huge space – physically, and with the roar of their collective voices.

I confess that, for me, that feeling of humility on approaching man-made structures on a grand scale is the same whether the space in question is secular or sacred. My heart soars as I stand beneath Michelangelo's dome at St Peter's Basilica in Rome, or contemplate the dramatic skyline silhouette of the Suleymaniye Mosque in Istanbul. And I feel similarly moved at the sight of the Guggenheim Museum in Bilbao, or as I wander down the massive ramp into the former turbine hall at Tate Modern in London.

For many in Britain, the image conjured up at the mention of 'great iconic buildings' is likely to be London's St Paul's Cathedral. The image in question may well be one, especially memorable one – the dome of the Cathedral illuminated by searchlights, during the night of 29 December 1940, at the height of the Blitz, in World War Two, captured by photographer Herbert Mason from the roof of the nearby *Daily Mail* building. Wreathed in billowing smoke, amidst the chaos and destruction of war, the pale dome stands proud and glorious – indomitable. At the height of that air-raid, Sir Winston Churchill telephoned the Guildhall to insist that all fire-fighting resources be directed at St Paul's. The cathedral must be saved, he said, whatever the cost to adjacent buildings. Damage to the fabric would sap the morale of the country.

Even before Churchill's intervention, the Cathedral authorities knew that the greatest threat to the survival of St Paul's was that of fire. It was decided to set up a company of fire-watchers, to keep watch for incendiary bombs. An appeal went out to the Royal Institute of British Architects for volunteers, and an astonishing roll-call of intellectuals responded. In addition to well-known architects, it included prominent figures from the arts like John Betjeman, and some of the most distinguished historians of the day. They kept vigil in shifts, nightly, sleeping in a command centre in the crypt. There is a wonderful 1942 photograph of them all, up on the roof of the Cathedral, posed awkwardly in rows in their tin hats, with their fire-fighting equipment laid out on the parapet in front of them.

In spite of their efforts, St Paul's did not in fact escape

unscathed. On 10 October 1940 a 500-pound bomb penetrated the choir, demolishing the high altar. Early in the morning of 17 April 1941 a direct hit on the north transept destroyed the vaulted roof over the crypt, punching a hole through the cathedral floor and causing quite shocking damage below. The mess was hastily cleared up and the damage to the fabric patched immediately, under the most difficult circumstances – most people never knew.

When I mentioned the bomb damage in a public lecture on Wren's St Paul's recently, a number of those in my audience were quite indignant that their cherished myth of the wartime indestructability of St Paul's should be thus challenged. But a lady in her late 60s came up to me afterwards to say that, the morning after the damage to the high altar, she had been carried, aged six, into the Cathedral on her fire-warden father's shoulders. 'Take a look and remember,' he told her. 'You will never, ever hear about this again.'

Arsenal's Highbury is to be preserved – its iconic status for football fans world-wide acknowledged by keeping intact the familiar East and West Stands, with their glorious art-deco iron- and plaster-work, ornament and lettering. A leading firm of architects, working closely with English Heritage, will transform the stadium into blocks of one- and two-bedroom apartments. The first residents will move in in 2008. The familiar outline of the pitch will stay too, recapitulated in the landscaping of an ornamental garden. No more studded boots on this turf, but an abiding memory of 93 years of passes, tackles and crucial free kicks.

Finding a new use for a redundant landmark building brilliantly serves a double purpose. It honours and celebrates the enduring sentiments a much-loved monument evokes, while once again making it a beacon for fresh activity – giving it back a purpose.

English Heritage recently launched a campaign, wittily entitled 'Inspired!', aimed at saving tens of thousands of places of worship nationwide which are in urgent need of repair. Many of these are parish churches. Most of them have dwindling congregations. English Heritage is sounding alarm-bells to warn us that the fabric of these much-loved local landmarks is in danger of deteriorating beyond hope of repair.

In their five-point plan to rescue much-loved landmarks across the British Isles, 'alternative use' for the buildings is treated as a desperate last measure. I think English Heritage needs to be bolder. On his way into the final game, one Arsenal football fan said of his beloved Highbury that, although he would no longer be cheering his team on in the Highbury stands: 'It's still a legacy, standing forever.' He had no qualms about celebrating his beloved Arsenal Stadium in its promised new incarnation.

I think English Heritage could count on a similarly upbeat attitude on the part of church congregations. They could encourage small congregations to combine with neighbouring parishes in a shared place of worship – after all, having to travel to a nearby village to use a bank or post a letter has been a reality of rural life for many years. A precious, listed parish church could then seek other sources of funding and be adapted to provide (for example) a congenial meeting place for all members of the community, a library, a performance space. Our hearts would still leap as we rounded a corner of the village green to find the church spire soaring above us, while worshippers would no longer need to worry about leaks in the roof.

After the Great Fire of London of 1666, a total of 86 City churches was destroyed. Times had changed, the Corporation of London decided, parishes could be consolidated. Only 39 City churches were included in the rebuilding plans. Proceeds from the sale of the sites of those churches not rebuilt and from the disposal of their churchyards were added to the Coal Tax revenue to provide more ample funds. The result was the sublime Wren masterpieces which remain the glory of the London cityscape today.

We need to think creatively today, if we are to preserve our architectural heritage. The first of those City churches to be embarked upon by Wren, in 1671, was St Nicholas Cole Abbey. The building was badly damaged in the Second World War, and subsequently entirely reconstructed. Today it stands empty and redundant. An ingenious architectural scheme has been proposed, creating a free-standing glass box inside the shell of the church, and transforming it into a set of attractive, airy spaces for educational uses. The church of St Nicholas Cole Abbey will acquire new life and new purpose. Like Arsenal's Highbury its beauty and grandeur will continue to arrest our attention and make our spirits soar. It will be filled with memories, rich in history, a source of inspiration for those who enter, for those who pause 'in awkward reverence', and for those who simply pass by.

Four

THE UNEXPECTED REAPPEARANCE IN EARLY 2006 OF LOST, HANDWRITTEN MINUTES OF MEETINGS OF THE ROYAL SOCIETY DATING FROM THE SEVENTEENTH CENTURY, WHICH HAD NEVER BEEN PROPERLY FILED IN THE SOCIETY'S ARCHIVES, LED ME TO CONSIDER THE IMPLICATIONS OF THE FACT THAT I HAVE NEVER BEEN MUCH GOOD AT ORGANISING MY PAPERWORK.

Some people actually enjoy filing and paperwork. I confess I am not one of them. Given the chance, I will always plunge with enthusiasm into a fresh activity, rather than pause to complete the records for the last one.

My negligence where paper is concerned bothers me, because, in my professional life as a historian, I know that my research relies upon the documents and records of past events, carefully preserved and systematically organised by others. They are the building-blocks of history. Meticulous minute-taking, monthly accounts and regular filing are an important part of the lasting fame of an individual, and the enduring life of any organisation.

I suspect this is one of the reasons why I am so attached to the seventeenth-century scientist Robert Hooke. We are, in this respect, all-too alike. He too preferred dashing around making things happen, and balked at providing the painstaking documentation afterwards.

Put in charge of essential paperwork for the Royal Society – Europe's leading scientific establishment at that time – he let the project slip badly. In fact, the Society is celebrating the retrieval of almost 600 long-lost pages from their early records, which Hooke failed to file in 1682.

Robert Hooke was born in 1635 and died in 1703. He was an outstanding hands-on experimentalist, observational astronomer, engineer, architect and instrument-maker. He was the first Curator of the newly-established Royal Society in London, an accomplished observer with telescopes and microscopes he built himself, a strong contender for discovering the inverse-square law of gravitational attraction, and the indefatigable surveyor responsible for measuring and pegging-out the street-plan of the City of London after the Great Fire. He discovered Hooke's Law of elasticity, and designed the universal joint still known by his name. He was Wren's close friend and Newton's great enemy (Hooke had dared to criticise some of Newton's early work, and was never forgiven for it).

The diarist Samuel Pepys – a great admirer of Hooke's scientific talents – described him as the man who 'is the most [impressive]' but 'promises the least, of any man in the world that ever I saw'. By that he meant that Hooke's appearance was a disappointment. He was nondescript, his slight build diminished further by a curvature of the spine. But his energy and ingenuity more than made up for his lack of personal presence.

Faced with a fresh intellectual or practical challenge – a novel experiment, something new to calculate, or to observe through his telescope, there was nothing Hooke would not undertake – he found it impossible to say no. Trying – and failing – to get Hooke to concentrate on a particular project in hand, the first President of the Society, Sir Robert Moray, complained: 'I easily believe Hooke has not been idle, but I could wish he had finished the tasks laid upon him.'

For five years, beginning in November 1677, Hooke was the Secretary of the Royal Society, responsible for all its paper records. It was a job he was keen to undertake. He had become convinced that the previous Secretary, Henry Oldenburg, had been systematically downplaying the contribution he, Hooke, was making to the Society's activities, damaging his international reputation and depriving him of due scientific credit. Hooke believed that Oldenburg had withheld vital confirmation of new discoveries he had made – like his use of a hair-spring to regulate a pocket-watch.

Oldenburg had put in place a stringent set of procedures to ensure that the activities of the Royal Society were properly recorded for posterity. Following his unexpected death in September 1677, his arrangements were adopted as standard practice by the Society.

These were the demanding clerking activities Hooke now

took on. He had to attend all meetings of the Society and its governing Council and take detailed minutes. Then he had to mark them up and pass them to the official scribes, for them to make fair copies for the record. All papers read at the meetings had to be entered in full; all correspondence received had to be answered and filed.

For five full years Hooke failed miserably at all of these tasks. Within months of taking on the job, his minutes were erratic. Sometimes he simply failed to hand them over for transcription. His handwriting became so bad that the scribes had to leave gaps for words they could not decipher, or for documents he had failed to provide. He was a poor correspondent, and an even worse filer of letters and drafts. He gave up entering the scientific papers altogether.

Given what else he was doing at the time, Hooke's less-than-adequate secretarial efforts are hardly surprising. The years of his Secretaryship coincided with the high-point of his involvement in the rebuilding of London. As City Surveyor he continued to adjudicate in all property disputes arising from alterations in street plans and building positions, including attending all court cases. As site architect for Sir Christopher Wren's office, he was responsible for several City churches and for structural work at St Paul's.

Even at the Royal Society, Hooke's secretarial responsibilities came on top of more pressing, practical duties. His principal job as Curator of Experiments obliged him to produce a weekly practical experiment to be demonstrated in front of the Fellows – a small bird to be suffocated in the vacuum-creating air-pump; a specimen of rain water to be examined under the microscope for wriggling protozoa invisible to the naked eye. Between meetings he was expected to investigate any scientific matters raised by members, in person or by correspondence, and to conduct further experiments.

Under all these competing pressures, his record-keeping duties were inevitably the first to suffer. Senior Royal Society officials became exasperated, and in November 1682 he was removed from the post of Secretary. The bundle of draft minutes, letters from notable scientists overseas, and scientific papers submitted by Fellows, which he should have lodged in the Society's archives, languished in his rooms at Gresham College, joining accumulating piles of his own unfinished working papers. After his death in 1703, loyal friends attempted to sort out Hooke's personal effects and to rationalise his piles of paper. Eventually they gave up.

Without those crucial documents, the files of the Royal Society were incomplete. A five-year hole yawned in their impeccably ordered records of their action-packed early years. Sequences of experiments and vital supporting documents were lost. The history of the Scientific Revolution was interrupted.

Then, out of the blue, in January of this year, the missing Hooke papers resurfaced. Removed from Hooke's lodgings by one of his executors, they had found their way to a country house in Hampshire, and languished there without anyone, apparently, realising their importance. Unearthed in the course of a routine valuation, the papers were offered for sale by Bonhams auctioneers, with a suggested price of one and a half million pounds.

The President of the Royal Society, Lord Rees, led a spirited public campaign to return the Hooke folio to its rightful place in the basement strong-room of the Society. In a nail-biting finale, the manuscript was secured for somewhat less than the asking price by the Society's negotiators, while the sale was actually in progress. The purchase by the Society was announced in the auction-room, where representatives of three overseas collectors were waiting with bids of – allegedly – up to four million pounds.

In late May, the papers were carried with great ceremony into a reception in the Society's grand premises in Carlton House Terrace, a stone's throw from Buckingham Palace. In the room were all those who had contributed to the fund – ordinary members of the public who had sent five and ten pound cheques, individual Fellows who had contributed larger sums, and representatives of the Wellcome Trust which had saved the day with half a million. The atmosphere was one of jubilation.

The Hooke folio will provide missing links in chains of discussion, experimentation and discovery which historians of science like myself can trace by diligently following the paper trails. I will be able to handle and study it on a daily basis. Eventually a team of researchers will digitise and transcribe the fragile manuscript, making it possible for everyone who cares to view and study it online. We must remember to archive the emails we send in the course of that project – in future those electronic exchanges will be the historian's raw materials.

The excitement surrounding the reappearance of the papers may finally have restored Hooke to his rightful place as a major figure in England's Scientific Revolution. But beyond that, its recovery also teaches people like myself a valuable lesson. Those of us who are not temperamentally inclined to keep on top of the paperwork had better look to our lasting reputations.

hospital. Fewer beds means more money elsewhere in the system and better satisfaction all round.

'Not so', countered the spokesperson from the health-workers' union UNISON. Entire wards have been closed under cost-cutting measures. 'Hot-bedding' (a patient being allocated a bed just vacated by somebody else) increases hospital infections like MRSA. Lobbing statistics back-and-forth between them, both stuck resolutely to their point of view.

How could one set of figures produce two such diametrically opposed arguments? Here was a good example of the fact that statistical data will always allow more than one interpretation. How we view the results will depend on our own attitudes and emotions as much as on the data.

Why are we so easily hoodwinked by numbers? We are much more sophisticated when it comes to words – we are not inclined to take the assertion that 'Guinness is good for you', or 'Persil washes whiter' entirely seriously. Women are particularly good at decoding the claims made by cosmetics advertising for new 'miracle' merchandise: this cream 'reverses the signs of ageing', that one 'guarantees instant radiance'. If we buy the beauty product it will probably be because of the packaging, or just to cheer ourselves up.

By contrast, we read our real hopes and fears into claims based on statistics. Advertisers know that an appeal to the aspirations and anxieties of a target audience can make for highly successful marketing. In April this year, the manufacturers of Head and Shoulders shampoo were reprimanded by the Advertising Standards Agency for claiming that their product 'leaves your hair 100 per cent dandruff free'. Dandruff sufferers imagined quite reasonably that if they used Head and Shoulders they would be able to snuggle up, without those tell-tale signs of flaking ruining the embrace.

But what the makers, Procter and Gamble, actually meant was that in trials, Head and Shoulders had reduced flaky scalp in 95 per cent of cases, so that the dandruff was not visible from a distance of 2 feet away. As for the 5 per cent whose scalps had not met even this level of improvement during the timescale of the trials – 'a few more weeks' use' would have done the trick.

While this kind of fiddling with the figures will probably be spotted, other, subtler deceptions can be more difficult to recognise. Since antiquity, word-games involving numbers have been used to teach non-logicians to appreciate the pitfalls of arguments based upon them.

The 'argument of the heap' – 'sorites' – was a favourite teaser of the ancient Greek philosophers. How big is a heap? Ask someone whether a handful of barley – say 50 grains – makes a heap. The answer, of course, is 'no'. Now ask: 'Well then, if you add a grain to your handful, are 50 grains plus one a heap? No? Then what about 51 plus one?' And so on. You are bound to reach the conclusion that no number of grains of barley, however large, ever becomes 'big' enough to be called a heap.

Incremental changes made to a large population produce no exact point at which we can say: 'That is now a heap.' Hence the paradox. Words like 'many' and 'few' lead us by unobjectionable stages to an unacceptable conclusion.

Even before the *Today* programme guests jolted me awake with their numbers paradox, another widely-covered piece of medical research had set me thinking about how we decide what counts as 'big' and 'small' likelihoods, to match our own circumstances.

Some weeks earlier, the *British Medical Journal* had announced the results of a study of the effect of the pattern of women's lives on their health. Newspapers seized on one set of statistics. 'Working mums less likely to be obese', the headlines yelled.

'Research suggests that staying at home and giving up work leads to poorer long-term health,' wrote the *Times* health correspondent. 'The risk of becoming obese was found to be almost double for a stay-at-home mother.'

I imagine that working mothers like myself smiled smugly and thought: 'Well at least we get a bonus from going out to work all our lives – it keeps us thin', while our home-making sisters sighed, and shook their heads at the thought that ending up overweight was yet another penalty for their decision to devote themselves to caring for the family.

The study had actually found that 38 per cent of women who did not go out to work were likely to become obese by middle age, compared with 23 per cent of women who did.

Of course, no journalist wants a headline that reads: 'A few more stay-at-home mothers put on weight, than those juggling jobs and family responsibilities'. Newspaper editors have to grab our attention, and precise-sounding figures apparently do that rather well. So the advertisement for a well-known after-shampoo conditioner, featuring a gorgeous brunette with shining tresses, proclaims: 'leaves your hair 4 times smoother!' And the ad for a new brand of mascara solemnly tells us that it makes eyelashes '15 times sexier' – whatever that might mean!

When a new cancer-treatment drug hit the headlines in 2005, the headline read: 'Herceptin halves the chance of breast cancer recurring'. It sounded like a miracle. Those, like myself, at that time recovering from surgery and the rigours of chemotherapy could have been forgiven for believing that this meant a 50 per cent reduction in their chance of ever getting breast cancer again, if only they could persuade their NHS trust to pay £20,000 for a course of treatment.

It took me a while to realise that, even though I was one of those suitable for treatment with Herceptin, nobody – not even the surgeon I most trusted and admired – could state unequivocally that taking the new drug would mean the end of all my fears. In fact, once again, the statistics could be interpreted in different ways depending on a person's circumstances and on their state of mind about their own medical prognosis.

In the first results from British trials of the new drug, just over 9 per cent of women found their cancer returned. For those who had not been given Herceptin, the recurrence rate was just over 17 per cent. For women like myself, who were temperamentally inclined to believe that their treatments thus far gave them a good chance of total recovery, the new drug seemed to promise a smallish reduction of an already lowish chance of their cancer returning. And this outcome could be matched by drugs which had been through exhaustive trials and had been demonstrated to have fewer potentially harmful side-effects.

On the other hand, those women who were most fearful – who already felt convinced that their cancer was bound to come back – were sure that Herceptin would cut that likelihood of recurrence in half. It would give them twice the chance of survival. They believed themselves destined to be in that unlucky group who would fall ill again, and they seized upon the pharmaceutical company's promotional claims as potential salvation. For them, getting Herceptin on the NHS was, as several of them have said publicly, a matter of life and death.

Working woman, dandruff-sufferer, recovering cancer patient, each of us tries to put the best interpretation we can on the figures, to suit ourselves. Meanwhile, health authorities trying to meet all needs and demands from a fixed pot of money, face a real dilemma. Should they pay for the cruelly expensive new chemical for all suitable patients, for the benefit of the most anxious, or are they entitled to argue that the 'cost per life saved' is simply too high?

Drugs like Herceptin can offer hope. But, as in the case of the 'heap' argument, there never comes a point at which we are able to say that the greater likelihood of survival is a 'cure'. So who is to arbitrate in these situations – who is to decide if the cost of prescribing it is justified?

We need informed debate – an ongoing dialogue with the medical profession. But if dialogue breaks down, we should not, in my view, take cases like these to the courts. When patients take their health-care provider to court, they are asking the law to 'take their side', to decide, in cases where the disagreement depends, in the end, not on the statistics, but on strong emotions. Statistics may give us the impression of objectivity, but our decisions based upon them are always, ultimately subjective.

Six

HOLLAND HAS HAD A REPUTATION FOR TOLERANCE SINCE THE SIXTEENTH CENTURY, SETTING AN EXAMPLE TO OTHER EUROPEAN COUNTRIES. BUT A SERIES OF SHOCKING EVENTS IN RECENT YEARS HAS SEEMED TO BE DRIVING THE DUTCH INTO UNCHARACTERISTICALLY HARD-LINE AND INTOLERANT POSITIONS ON IMMIGRATION AND DIVERSITY. ONE OF THESE EVENTS INVOLVED A YOUNG MUSLIM WOMAN FROM SOMALIA, WHO WAS FIRST EMBRACED AND THEN REJECTED BY THE DUTCH PUBLIC. THE FURORE SURROUNDING HER SITUATION REACHED BOILING POINT IN JUNE 2006.

There are times when a small event raises an issue of enormous importance. Ayaan Hirsi Ali, the Somali-born politician and women's rights activist, is leaving Holland for good.

You may never have heard of her, I will tell you more about

her in a moment. It is a strange irony that a country which has for centuries welcomed all those fleeing persecution should find it impossible to continue to provide Hirsi Ali with a refuge.

The Dutch have had a reputation for tolerance for almost five hundred years. By the 1500s the Dutch writer and educationalist Erasmus of Rotterdam was already disseminating broadmindedness and inclusion to the whole of the western world through his Latin treatises and textbooks.

In July 1572, the Protestant leader of the northern Netherlands, William I of Orange, still celebrated today as the Father of the Dutch nation, publicly proclaimed the right of all individuals to freedom of thought and worship at a political assembly at Dordrecht. William the Silent (as he was known affectionately to his people, because of his inscrutability) vowed 'to protect and preserve the country from foreign tyrants and oppressors', and he promised the Dutch people that 'the free exercise of religion should be allowed as well to Papists as Protestants, without any molestation or impediment'.

When, a month later, Catholic France turned on her own Protestants, and tens of thousands of Calvinist Huguenots were brutally murdered in the St Bartholomew's Day massacre, it was Holland which took in large numbers of the ensuing flood of refugees. It was Holland, too, which for centuries welcomed the Jews, displaced from all over Europe by Christian persecution.

Holland's immigrants have played a vital part in her rise to power and wealth – skilled Huguenot artisans were the motor behind Dutch clock- and instrument-making, Jewish commercial acumen helped build the Dutch East India Company. Artists and musicians from the two communities made rich contributions to the Golden Age of Dutch culture. Holland became famous for her diversity, her intermingled lifestyles and variety, an object lesson to the rest of Europe in how tolerance could build a stronger nation.

Again in the 1950s, Holland offered a European home to immigrants from the former Dutch colonies – Surinam, Indonesia and the Moluccas. From the 1960s onwards it was Moroccan Muslims who were drawn to the Netherlands by her booming economy. As the pace of immigration quickened across Europe, the Dutch remained steadfast in their historic commitment to open borders and in their readiness to accept and tolerate difference. By the beginning of the twenty-first century more than 10 per cent of Holland's population of 16.3 million were 'non-Western' immigrants. Close to one million of these are Muslims.

You can feel Holland's extraordinary diversity as you walk through the commercial district of any Dutch town. Amsterdam, Rotterdam and Delft are melting pots of cultures and creeds, bustling with energy and excitement.

The assassination in 2002 of the right-wing, anti-immigrant politician Pim Fortuyn was a rude awakening for many among the broadly open-minded Dutch. It was a loss of innocence – a looking up and seeing as if for the first time (as the French did during the riots in the Paris suburbs at the end of 2005) the ghettos in the suburbs, high immigrant unemployment, disenchanted youth and downtrodden Muslim women.

The murder of filmmaker Theo van Gogh in 2004 by a Dutch-born Islamic extremist sent a second traumatic shock-wave through the nation. Van Gogh was attacked as he cycled through central Amsterdam, and savagely killed in front of horrified bystanders. His attacker impaled a five-page written statement on van Gogh's body declaring the killing an act of retribution for a film van Gogh had made to draw attention to the abuse of women within the immigrant Islamic community.

Most of the accusations in the letter pinned to van Gogh's chest were aimed at his collaborator and screenwriter, Ayaan Hirsi Ali.

Hirsi Ali arrived in Holland as an asylum-seeker in 1992, claiming to be fleeing a forced marriage. There she campaigned tirelessly to draw attention to the abuses suffered by Holland's deprived Islamic women. In 2003 she became a member of Parliament for the Dutch Liberal Party, and successfully raised the profile of her cause, earning widespread admiration. She attracted fierce anger, however, from radical elements in the immigrant Islamic community.

On the day of Theo van Gogh's murder, Hirsi Ali was forced into hiding. Ever since, she has had to have constant police protection, and has been forced into an increasingly lonely isolation, ostensibly for her own safety. Cut off from normal conversation and political debate, she has become an embarrassment, and, finally, an annoyance to many of the Dutch liberals who once supported her. Earlier this year she moved into a high-security apartment block, but was obliged to leave again, when her neighbours petitioned to have her evicted, because of fears that her presence put them at risk.

In May, Ayaan Hirsi Ali resigned from the Dutch

Parliament. In the face of a growing clamour from both the Muslim and the secular communities to silence her, she had decided to re-settle in Washington. Now, in spite of her imminent departure, she has been told by the Immigration Minister, Rita Verdonk, that she is to be stripped of her Dutch citizenship because – out of fear – she did not use her real family name on her original application for asylum.

Since taking office in 2003, Verdonk has ordered citizenship tests for immigrants, raised visa fees by hundreds of euros and has begun imprisoning failed asylum-seekers before deporting them. She has shown herself resolutely hard-line in a number of other high-profile immigration cases – including refusing to fast-track the citizenship application of Ivory-Coast soccer player Salomon Kalou to allow him to play for Holland in the World Cup. Verdonk intends to run for Prime Minister in next year's elections. Dutch popular opinion appears to be running her way.

What are we to think of all of this? I have heard several comments to the effect that Holland has 'at last got her come-uppance', as if the Dutch were the last Europeans to understand that a long-standing tradition of easy-going liberal tolerance had finally come to an end under the pressure of global migration and post-9/11 polarisation in the 'war on terror'.

But this is surely the wrong way to look at this sequence of events. The cutting down of an individual with a flamboyant voice and message (Fortuyn was openly gay, van Gogh was a maverick media polemicist) strikes a direct, targeted blow against the values of liberal western nations. Beyond the random terror of hijackings and bombs, it is deliberately aimed at freedom of speech – at our right to express our views in public, whether or not they are the views of the majority, without fear of reprisal. We should all be concerned at the way violence in the Netherlands has produced a back-lash against the open expression of dissenting or unconventional views.

Holland is the canary in the mine-shaft. As we in Britain watch with fascination, the Dutch Left and Right appear to be coming together in maintaining that immigration barriers have to be put in place, and hard-line legislation enacted to control forcibly those who are already there – exactly as is happening in other, less historically-openminded European countries like our own. When the Dutch canary stops singing, we should beware. It will tell us that we have sacrificed personal liberty and freedom of speech out of fear of assassination on some street corner in broad daylight.

It is not easy to resist the urge to quiet an irritant voice like Hirsi Ali's. But each of us has to understand that the price of communal silence – the decision not to talk openly about difficult-to-resolve issues of faith and mores – is too high for us to pay. Tolerance is a two-way street, and negotiating its traffic requires continuous, open dialogue. The cut and thrust of political debate, public controversy, and stated positions unacceptable to particular groups, is a vital part of a healthy political state.

Twelve years after his Dordrecht speech, William the Silent was assassinated in his own home by Balthasar Gérard, a fanatical Catholic, who had inveigled his way into William's Delft headquarters with a new-fangled wheel-lock pistol concealed in his sleeve – his deadly act the sixteenth-century equivalent of a suicide-bombing. The northern Netherlands reeled, the ruling élite closed ranks; repressive political measures were taken.

Eventually, though, the States General recovered their Erasmian principles and shook off the fear and blind panic which had followed the calamitous event. The values William of Orange had fought for were too precious – too fundamental – to be discarded lightly.

Seven

IN EARLY SUMMER 2006 A LONG-RUNNING DISPUTE OVER PAY BETWEEN UNIVERSITY ACADEMICS AND UNIVERSITY VICE-CHANCELLORS FINALLY REACHED A SETTLEMENT. THE MEDIA APPEARED TO BE PRETTY UNINTERESTED IN THE WORKING CONDITIONS OF ACADEMICS, OR INDEED IN THE UNIVERSITIES IN GENERAL. AN INSPIRING EVENT ORGANISED BY MY OWN GRADUATE STUDENTS PROMPTED ME TO PLEAD THE CASE FOR GREATER PUBLIC SUPPORT FOR HIGHER EDUCATION IN BRITAIN.

One weekend in June, as the grey skies lifted and the sun finally came out, when most people were heading for the park, I spent a spell-binding day indoors instead, looking into the future of academic research in the humanities. I was taking part in a one-day conference at Queen Mary, University of London, organised by young colleagues in the Centre for

Editing Lives and Letters, where I am the Director. Students in their second and third year of post-graduate study made short presentations, to which senior academic 'mentors' responded with comments and advice. We ended the day eating supper together under the trees in the fading light, on the terrace of Queen Mary's award-winning graduate building in Mile End, beside the Regent's canal.

The topics were varied, but they shared an overarching theme. Armed with awesome specialist skills – palaeography (that's how to read long-obsolete handwritings), descriptive bibliography (how the pages of old books are put together), Latin and Greek – each student described a unique encounter in the archives with a piece of evidence which had changed their way of thinking about a significant issue in their field.

To take one example: in the Wren Library in Cambridge, a student had found a small book in Latin on the art of translation, published in 1559 in Basle by an exiled Protestant Englishman. An absolutely tiny printed book, with the tiniest of tiny handwriting in it less than half a millimetre high. It had been densely annotated in Latin by someone called Gabriel Harvey – for a short time in the 1570s the Cambridge University Professor of Rhetoric, and a man prominent in literary life in England for the next two decades. He had inscribed his name on the title page, and the date – 1570 – when he began reading it.

By looking at Harvey's marginal notes, the student had recovered an animated debate between reader and author about how imaginative and free one was entitled to be in turning a text from an ancient language into a modern one.

It is a debate intensely relevant to English religious politics of the time, centred as that was on the translation and inter-pretation of the Bible.

The student presented her book, its handwritten annota-tions and their analysis, with infectious enthusiasm, moving confidently with her laser-pointer between electronic images of its pages. She shared with us her detective work figuring out the significance of the red chalk marks for emphasis, the underlinings, and curious crossings-out. She singled out telling remarks by the annotator – in his distinctive black ink and minute italic hand. Sometimes, she showed us, he scribbled those comments so fast, with such eagerness to get on, that its mirror-image can still be seen, blotted on to the facing page before the ink dried, as he hurried to turn over.

This pint-sized book, she pointed out, does not figure in the latest, much-used, electronic resource for historians of the English literary heritage, which only reproduces books in English. Yet her little treasure-trove volume with its evocative annotations showed that it was an integral part of early Anglican doctrinal developments – still the guiding princi-ples of the Church of England today.

This is the way academic research in the humanities is meant to be, I believe, in the twenty-first century: engaged with real issues, alert, alive, and full of energy. Here is intel-lectual athleticism, leading to skills that can be transferred without difficulty to today's fast-moving world: how to iden-tify a significant problem, the sustained analysis of bodies of difficult data, rapid processing of information, and confident arrival at valid conclusions supported by telling evidence.

How ridiculously far all of this feels from recent press

comments, during the stand-off between beleaguered university Vice-Chancellors and harassed and exasperated university lecturers.

You may hardly have been aware at all, that for months some lecturers at universities have been taking part in 'action short of a strike', in support of a 23 per cent pay claim. They argued that their salaries have fallen well behind those of comparable public sector professionals and that a significant adjustment was necessary to enable them to 'catch up'. Their action consisted in withholding marks for the assessment of student coursework, and refusing to set and mark examinations. They have now reluctantly accepted a lower offer from the Vice-Chancellors of 13 per cent over three years.

Throughout the dispute, the public's attitude has hovered somewhere between lack of interest and lack of concern. Few contest the fact that academic salaries have fallen far behind those of most other professions. Yet no-one seemed to be terribly bothered as to whether academics were adequately rewarded for educating the next generation of intellectual high-flyers. The lecturers' continuing action reached the headlines only occasionally, when somebody noticed that it might have knock-on consequences for students' careers.

Why do the British have so little respect for their academics? We are constantly being told that our future is as a knowledge-based economy. That means we will need a better and more broadly educated workforce, made up of those who can argue a case coherently, appraise, analyse and evaluate. Which in turn means a longer, more challenging programme of education – more students in the sixth form, more undergraduates, more PhDs.

The BBC website currently contains an education correspondent's disparaging comments, suggesting that the failure
of universities to resolve their pay dispute typifies the point-
lessness of all academic endeavour. According to him, it is
no surprise that the two sides were not able to agree over
basic facts such as the average pay of lecturers, what the
universities could afford in the way of settlement, or even the
date the dispute had begun. 'Academic discourse often
descends into vitriolic disagreement over what is, or is not,
a "fact",' he writes scathingly.

I find such trivialising of the value of what we academics
do and contribute, deeply depressing, and wide of the mark.
Talking about the challenge of globalisation recently on the
Today programme, Gordon Brown told John Humphrys
emphatically that we need to invest more in education if we
are to meet the global economic challenge. We need to make
our universities more competitive, said Brown, we need more
scientists to meet that challenge. As the Chancellor knows full
well, there are significant costs attached to those ambitions.

Gordon Brown's clarion call reminded me of remarks a
couple of years ago by the then Education Minister: 'I don't
mind there being some medievalists around for ornamental
purposes', he said, 'but there is no reason for the state to pay
for them.' If we are to be 'one of the great global success
stories of the twenty-first century', we need investment in the
university sector right across the board. We will need more
highly educated young people in every discipline if we are to
keep pace with change. The kinds of students I train will be
every bit as valuable to the new-style British economy as physicists or even engineers.

One of my most gifted young researchers gave up her research post last year, and has just qualified as a schoolteacher. Her reasons were clear, and I wholeheartedly supported her: teachers in Britain's schools now have a proper career structure, and good conditions of service. Significant investment since 1997 means that schoolteaching now offers realistic and fair remuneration. Schoolteachers have begun to regain their position of respect in the community, and with it their own self-respect. At the graduate-organised conference I described above, she rushed up to tell me that she had just got a job at a well-known London girls' secondary school.

I have watched that student teach Shakespeare to a large class of first-year undergraduates. She is an inspiration in the classroom – one of those individuals who can control a lively group and communicate effectively without ever raising her voice. Her decision to leave a promising career in higher education is secondary education's gain. But it speaks volumes for this country's failure to value its universities. At a time when our universities are more important to us than ever before, we are in danger of destroying them by simple neglect.

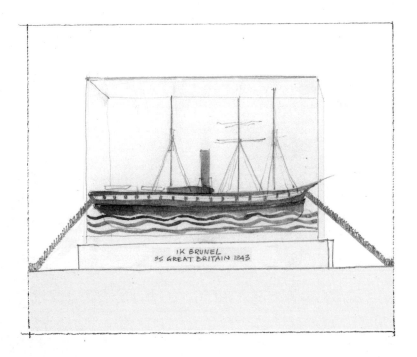

IK BRUNEL
SS GREAT BRITAIN 1843

and Curators have learned that the public needs to be entertained as well as enlightened. When I visited the newly restored SS *Great Britain* in Bristol recently – the world's first iron-hulled, steam-powered ocean going ship, designed and built by Britain's favourite engineer, Isambard Kingdom Brunel, in 1843, and now a crowd-pulling museum – the atmosphere was festive. Brunel himself would have been delighted.

Brunel's visionary idea was that the SS *Great Britain* would be the culmination of an entirely new travel experience. Adventurous Victorians would take the new Great Western Railway from London to Bristol, crossing Brunel's majestic Maidenhead Bridge over the Thames, hurrying over his 65 foot high Wharncliffe viaduct spanning the Brent valley, and thundering downhill through the two-mile-long Box Tunnel between Swindon and Bath. Having reached Bristol they would embark for New York aboard his state-of-the-art iron ship – and indeed, the SS *Great Britain*'s maiden voyage, completed in an astounding 14 days, marked the beginning of reliable and efficient transatlantic passenger travel (though on that record-breaking occasion it set out from Liverpool).

The renovated and restored SS *Great Britain* won the 2006 prestigious Gulbenkian museum of the year award, and deservedly so. The ship has been lovingly restored to the way it was in its heyday, with such flair and imagination that the experience of sailing on it has been vividly recaptured. 'It never feels like a museum at all', was one visitor's comment. 'The ship is allowed to speak for itself.' A brilliant illusion has been created with running water over glass plates, giving the impression that the ship – actually in a restored dry-dock – is afloat. After touring the interior – marvelling at the

beautifully crafted mahogany fixtures and fittings in the
elegant first-class cabins, inspecting the galley, and taking a
peek into the ingeniously compact 'conveniences' – you
descend beneath the water line to admire the extraordinary
iron hull and giant screw propeller as if from the sea floor,
the ship towering above you, dwarfing you into insignificance.

In mid-June, leading museum organisations celebrated ten
years of what they call 'spectacular' achievements by Britain's
providers of cultural enlightenment and diversion. Their joint
statement, under the upbeat title, 'Values and Vision', pledged
further efforts to broaden and increase the attractiveness of
what is on offer. If the Government will just continue current
levels of support, they will deliver ever more exciting exhibi-
tions and performances. Currently 25 million of us visit a
museum at least once a year. That figure, they promise, will
increase still further, 'placing audiences at the centre of what
[museums and galleries] do'.

But concentrating on visitor numbers and access has curious consequences for the future of the wonderfully diverse
array of museums and galleries across the country – from the
architecturally spectacular Lowry in Manchester to the serene,
cliff-top Tate St Ives in Cornwall.

Museums were not originally designed to draw crowds.
They were private accumulations of fascinating exotica,
assembled with private money for rich men's benefit: expensive, exclusive and largely inaccessible to the general public.

The London physician Hans Sloane (later Sir Hans), for
instance, was already an amateur collector of pressed botanical specimens and curiosities when, in 1687, he was asked
to join the household of the newly-appointed governor of

Jamaica, as his personal physician. Sloane was immediately attracted by the opportunities the post would afford him as a botanical enthusiast. As he told fellow-naturalist John Ray: 'Next to the serving of his grace and family in my profession, my business [will be] to see what I can meet withall that is extraordinary in nature in those places'. He accepted the job.

The party reached Jamaica in December 1687, after nearly three months at sea, and Sloane immediately began to assemble a comprehensive collection of local botanical, entomological and zoological specimens. He pressed the plants and smaller insects between large sheets of brown paper, preserving larger, fleshier items in jars of alcohol. He had those he could not preserve immortalised in pen and ink by local artists.

'When I return'd to England' (he wrote later) 'I brought with me about 800 Plants, most whereof were New, [and] shew'd them very freely to all lovers of such Curiosities'. Showing them 'very freely' meant allowing other gentlemen of his acquaintance to admire his specimens.

A mere year after Sloane and the governor had set sail from England, his eminent patient died. Sloane's last duty as his physician was to use his by now considerable skills as a preserver of specimens to embalm his body for shipment home to England.

Sloane never embarked on a comparable adventure again. But he continued to build his collections while he pursued a successful career as a society doctor in London. The funds at his disposal were further enhanced by the fortune he made marketing a product he had brought back from Jamaica – medicinal drinking chocolate.

Sloane describes in his *Natural History* how he hit upon the idea. In Jamaica chocolate was regarded as having therapeutic value for the digestion. Sloane's brainwave was to mix the bitter-tasting raw chocolate with warm milk and sugar and sell it as a remedy for stomach ailments.

The proceeds of 'Sloane's milk chocolate' funded his consuming passion for collecting. By the end of his life, Sloane had bought up practically every major botanical collection, 'dried garden' and cabinet of curiosities in the country – purchasing from any fellow-collector who was prepared to relinquish his treasures for cash, and outbidding all competitors at auction.

Sloane's collection of specimens from all over the globe was eventually so large that he didn't have space to unpack some of his purchases from the cases in which they arrived. It comprised 71,000 objects, a herbarium and a library of thousands of books and manuscripts. In 1752 he offered them all to King George II, for £20,000 – a knock-down price, he maintained, only a quarter of its actual value. A public lottery was organised to raise the asking price, and the following year the British Museum was born.

The founding collections of specimens in the British Museum are, then, the product of one man's idiosyncratic interests, expanded more or less haphazardly. Whatever Sloane fancied, he bought.

But Sloane's idea of making his extraordinary collection available to the public was not quite what we would understand today. Entry to the new British Museum was to be given to 'all studious and curious Persons'. You had to apply to the porter for a ticket. Unsuitable applicants were politely turned away. If a request to visit was accepted, after a period of weeks, you were permitted to participate in a closely supervised two-hour guided tour.

So how are our modern museums to cope with the fact that almost all their funding now has to go towards driving those visitor numbers ever upwards, to guarantee Government support?

Wealthy collectors like Sloane paid for their habit out of their own deep pockets, from which also came the essential finances for conservation, display and renewed acquisition. The custodians of our museums and galleries today – whether they are national, metropolitan ones, provincial centres, or attached to universities – have the same responsibility to conserve their collections, and keep them up to date by adding important new items. In many cases this is built into their foundation charter, trust document or ordinances. The dilemma for them is: more visitors, or preserving our museum heritage? That is the conundrum the signatories to the 'Value and Vision' pledge have to solve.

Entrepreneurialism and 'bling' have always been the basis for the private collector's compulsive collecting. We should look to the new rich to help us ensure our museums and galleries are fit for the future. Today's must-have item, snapped up by supermarket heirs and footballers' wives will be tomorrow's priceless museum treasure.

At a recent auction of items which had belonged to Princess Margaret, sold by her children to settle death duties, a bidder from China acquired the Poltimore Tiara, which the Princess wore at her wedding, for almost a million pounds. Just as Sloane spent his new-found wealth on beetles and butterflies, those made enormously rich by China's new commercial success are pouring theirs into their own pet passions. It is they, surely, who will furnish the world's museums and galleries with the next generation's items at which to ogle. Let us hope Museum Directors worldwide are already courting them.

Nine

ART AND ANCIENT ARTEFACTS HAVE ALWAYS PROVED ESPECIALLY VULNERABLE IN TIMES OF CONFLICT, AS THE SPOILS OF WAR REMOVED BY THE VICTOR AND CARRIED AWAY TO BE DISPLAYED IN TRIUMPH TO THE VICTORIOUS NATION. IN THE WEEK IN JUNE 2006 IN WHICH A LONG-LOST MASTERPIECE BY THE AUSTRIAN ARTIST EGON SCHIELE, WENT UP FOR AUCTION IN LONDON, I REFLECTED ON THE EQUIVALENT ACTS OF PLUNDER STILL BEING CARRIED OUT TODAY.

In mid-June, I went to look at a painting at Christie's auction house by the early-twentieth century Austrian artist Egon Schiele. The painting in question, 'Wilted Sunflowers', is a largish landscape – about a metre square. In the foreground are half a dozen tall, withered sunflower stems, silhouetted against distant, daisy-covered hills. Framed by dying leaves, the blackened sunflower heads droop heavily. Behind them the autumnal air is pale, and a white sun struggles through a wall of grey-brown mist. Painted in 1914, the work is considered to be a sombre homage to Van Gogh's 'Sunflowers'. It hints at decay, and the looming loss and destruction of the First World War.

This is a melancholy painting with a dark history. In the 1930s it belonged to the collector Karl Grünwald, a Viennese art and antiques dealer. During the First World War Grünwald and Schiele had served in the army together, and Grünwald, recognising the younger man's artistic talents, lobbied successfully to have him appointed as a war artist, rather than being sent to the front. Schiele died of influenza in 1918.

In 1938, the year Hitler annexed Austria, Grünwald fled to Paris. His finest art works were packed up to follow him, but they were intercepted in Strasburg, and auctioned off by the Nazis in 1942. Grünwald himself survived, but his wife and a daughter died in a concentration camp. After the war, first Karl Grünwald and then his son devoted much time, money and energy to searching for the stolen art works, with small success. Then, a year ago, 'Wilted Sunflowers' resurfaced in France. On Tuesday, the painting was sold to an anonymous buyer for an astounding 11.8 million pounds, the money going to Grünwald's heirs, closing a sad chapter in the family's history.

War and the pillaging of art and antiquities have always gone hand in hand. The callous accumulation by the Nazis of looted fine-art, in the form of personal possessions seized from Jews, many of whom were rounded up and sent to the gas chambers, is a shameful story of our time. But it is only one of the most recent and high-profile historical examples of the glories of a nation taken by force by its invaders.

The treaty of Campo Formio, signed in October 1797, marked the successful conclusion to Napoleon Bonaparte's campaigns in Italy and the end of the first phase of the Napoleonic Wars. As Imperial victor, Napoleon considered himself entitled to strip all his conquered Italian territories of their cultural and artistic treasures. 'Rome is no longer in Rome,' he is said to have announced exultantly. 'The whole of Rome is in Paris.'

The following year, Napoleon brought his trophies triumphantly back to France. A spectacular cavalcade wound its way through the streets of Paris, while crowds lined the route. Antique statuary including the great marble figure of the priest Laocoon (struggling with sea-snakes) and the majestic Roman Apollo Belvedere, with famous paintings by Raphaël, Titian and Tintoretto, all crammed into huge packing cases, were carried into the city on horse-drawn carts. To add to the sense of occasion, there were also animals from Napoleon's African campaign – a caged lion and a pair of dromedaries. But the parade's centre-piece was a cart bearing – unwrapped and on display – the four huge, antique, gilded bronze horses, which for 600 years had stood high above the great central door of St Mark's basilica in Venice.

In 1808 the Venetian horses provided the crowning glory for the Triumphal Arch erected by Napoleon in the Place du Carrousel, just in front of the Louvre. Today that arch still presides magnificently over one end of a nine-kilometre-long grand axis or vista, running through the Place de La Concorde, and the length of the Champs-Elysée, down to the better-known Arc de Triomphe.

The traffic in priceless antiquities, from defenceless to more powerful nations, continues today. Only today the perpetrators of the destruction of a nation's ancient heritage may well be its own people, enticed into selling off their patrimony to the highest bidder, out of the simple need to survive.

Plundering the vanquished, sacking conquered cities, and other such acts of war-related pillaging have occurred throughout history. Till now, though, they have followed a kind of inexorable logic. With the ebb and flow of empires, significant items stolen from one nation have been returned, or moved on, as new players enter the imperial scene. The bronze horses Napoleon removed from St Mark's basilica and took to Paris, had themselves been looted by Crusaders and brought to Venice after the sack of Constantinople six hundred years earlier. And in 1815, as Napoleon's power waned and he tried to curry favour with the Italians, he returned the horses to Venice, replacing them on the Carrousel arch with casts of the originals.

There is something much more brutally nihilistic about today's cultural theft. The succession of wars in modern Afghanistan has made its ancient archaeological sites acutely vulnerable to plunder, for objects to sell on the international black market. The squandering of Afghanistan's heritage began under the Taliban, when Mujahideen soldiers systematically ransacked the National Museum in Kabul, passing its contents on – often to order – to dealers in Pakistan and elsewhere. According to the Minister for Culture of the present, post-Taliban government, 90 per cent of the museum's collection was lost. Ivories, statues, paintings, coins, gold, pottery and armaments from the prehistoric periods onwards, are gone for ever.

What is now reaching the West from Afghanistan, however, is not museum exhibits, but recently excavated archaeological treasures. Since the fall of the Taliban, Afghanistan has become a grave-robber's paradise. The country's more than 3,000 historical sites are being systematically plundered. Experts estimate that there is not an ancient site left in the whole country that has not been partly or fully looted, with the contraband antiquities going to London, Tokyo and New York. As Afghanistan struggles to restore internal order and security, its rich, ancient past is seeping away, like sand between the fingers. As a Unesco spokesman puts it: 'To Afghan farmers, digging up antiquities is the same as digging up potatoes – you harvest what you can, so that your family can eat.'

Earlier this year it was reported that almost 4 tons of illegally acquired ancient Afghan artefacts had been seized here in Britain. They included ceramics, stone sculptures, Buddhist statues, bronze weapons and coins, dating back to the third century BC. At present these are stored for safety at the British Museum while discussions take place between the Foreign Office and the Afghan government over what to do with them.

Following the invasion of Iraq, the world watched in horror as the National Museum in Baghdad – left vulnerable and unguarded – was ransacked by looters, who removed any artefact that could be carried away, and destroyed or damaged many more in situ. American troops posted to protect the nearby Oil Ministry and its documents – judged crucial for the functioning of Iraq's oil industry – did nothing.

What is now Iraq was once the cradle of civilisation. The astonishing remains of its ancient peoples are an important part of our western civilisation. Amid the disorder of war they became the West's responsibility. How could we have failed to protect Iraq's unique and precious cultural heritage?

Some commodities on which the West depends, which are currently being rapidly depleted by uncontrolled western consumption, can, over time, be replaced. By the time readily accessible sources of affordable oil have been exhausted, economic necessity will surely have driven the developed world to discover some viable alternative.

Schiele's 'Wilted sunflowers', although lost for 70 years, was eventually recovered. Although its legitimate owner died without having located this, his best-loved painting, at least his family has now had satisfaction on his behalf.

The same cannot be said of the archaeological treasures currently pouring out of sites across Iraq and Afghanistan. The precious remains of peoples and practices long gone, some of which have survived for more than two millennia, are being removed undocumented from unexcavated sites, dispersed and squandered. Once plundered, they are lost for ever from history. And with them vanishes the collective memory of an entire civilisation.

Ten

I JULY 2005 MARKED THE NINETIETH ANNIVERSARY OF THE BATTLE OF THE SOMME. I WAS DETERMINED TO MAKE THAT ANNIVERSARY THE SUBJECT OF MY TALK FOR THE WEEK, BUT ALSO AWARE THAT THERE WOULD BE AN ENORMOUS AMOUNT OF OTHER COVERAGE IN THE MEDIA. STILL, IT WAS, I BELIEVED, NOT COMMON KNOWLEDGE THAT THE AUTHOR OF THAT EPIC WORK OF FICTION, *THE LORD OF THE RINGS*, J. R. R. TOLKIEN, WAS ONE OF THE YOUNG SOLDIERS WHO SURVIVED THE CARNAGE OF THAT MOST BLOODY OF BATTLES.

It is ninety years since Allied commanders launched the First World War offensive lastingly remembered as the Battle of the Somme. At 7.30 am on 1 July 1916, officers blew their whistles to signal the start of the attack. As eleven British divisions clambered out of their trenches and walked slowly towards the enemy lines, German machine guns opened fire, causing wholesale carnage.

The first day of the Battle was the bloodiest in the whole history of the British Army. By the end of that day, the British had suffered 60,000 casualties; almost 20,000 were dead. Sixty per cent of all officers involved on that first day were killed.

One of those who survived that horrific first assault, and who endured the prolonged ghastliness of the months of fighting that followed, was the young J. R. R. Tolkien.

The Allied plan had been to launch a coordinated Anglo-French assault. The British would attack along a 15-mile front north of the meandering river Somme. Five French divisions would attack along an eight-mile front through rolling farmland south of the Somme. To ensure a rapid advance with minimal resistance, Allied artillery had been pounding German lines for a week beforehand, firing over a million and a half shells at the enemy. British soldiers recalled later how throughout the night before the battle, the entire length of the Allied trenches shuddered and vibrated from the reverberating shock waves of uninterrupted big gun bombardment of the enemy lines.

The saturation bombardment was supposed to annihilate the opposing forces, leaving their positions undefended. Cavalry units would then pour through to pursue the fleeing Germans. But open preparations for the assault gave clear advance warning of an impending attack, and German troops simply moved into underground concrete bunkers and waited.

Almost five months later, the Allies had advanced only 5 miles, at a cost of over half a million lives. Early in 1917 the Germans fell back from their positions for strategic reasons.

Their withdrawal made a mockery of the months of bitter battle and appalling loss of life. It had all been for 'a few acres of mud'. Intended to be a decisive breakthrough, the Battle of the Somme instead became a byword for futile and indiscriminate slaughter.

At the Somme, the new, devastatingly efficient weapons of mass destruction – the tank, mustard-gas and the machine gun – marked the beginning of mechanised warfare on a huge scale. War would never be the same again.

The poet Wilfred Owen was killed in the final week of the First World War at the age of 25. His poems, which I first read at school, offer searing testimony to the way this new kind of war ended any possibility of romanticising personal sacrifice, or elevating the individual in combat to the status of hero. For me his 'Anthem for Doomed Youth' captures better than any military history an absolute disenchantment, no matter how 'good and true' the cause:

> What passing-bells for these who die as cattle?
> —Only the monstrous anger of the guns.
> Only the stuttering rifles' rapid rattle
> Can patter out their hasty orisons.

A more mundane kind of eye-witness account – but as compelling – comes from an extraordinary collection of audio-recordings of the recollections of ordinary serving soldiers, to be found on the Imperial War Museum website as part of their vivid 'virtual' Somme commemoration.

Private Don Murray, for instance, recalls how, as he and his comrades walked towards the enemy lines, the Germans appeared from their bunkers: 'They just wound up their guns on automatic affairs and fired . . ., and of course they just mowed us down.'

And he goes on to evoke the sense of numbing isolation, still vivid to him all those years later: 'And it seemed to me eventually there was just one man left, I couldn't see anybody at all, all I could see was men lying dead, men screaming, . . . and I thought what can I do, I was just alone in a hell of fire and smoke and stink.'

J. R. R. Tolkien had just graduated from Oxford with a first class degree in literature when he saw his first active service at the Somme. From July 1916 until he was invalided out with trench fever at the end of October, he experienced the full relentless ghastliness of day after day of trench life under fire – the discomfort, the cold, the mud, the lice, the fear, the unspeakable horrors witnessed.

He had taken comfort from the fact that he was fighting alongside his three oldest and dearest friends from his schooldays – a quartet of gifted would-be-poets who hoped to become outstanding literary men. But by November, two of those friends were dead. Tolkien and the one other surviving member of their 'Club' were never able to rebuild a closeness shattered by the enormity of what had occurred – by the sense of total loss, the obliteration of the band of friends almost before their creative lives had begun. As Tolkien's best friend, Geoffrey Bache Smith wrote, shortly after the death of the first of their number on 17 July: 'I am safe but what does that matter? . . . Now one realises in despair what [the Club] really was. . . . What ever are we going to do?' Within months Geoffrey too was dead.

Imagination is a uniquely human attribute. Freely exercised, it allows each of us to transform our everyday experience, elevating it into something more consolingly meaningful. How, then, does the human imagination cope with trauma of the kind Tolkien and his fellow-soldiers experienced in 1916?

We might expect those months of unremitting horror in the trenches of the Somme to have fed into, and coloured, the ferocious battles and scenes of slaughter in Tolkien's three-part *The Lord of the Rings* (begun in the 1930s), or in the 'Fall of Gondolin' story which he began writing while convalescing in the spring of 1917.

Glimpses of the battlefield do occur within Tolkien's epic tapestry: Morgoth's monstrous iron dragons surely owe something to the tanks first used in combat in the First World War, which terrified the horses of the cavalry. When he describes the desolation of the battlefield, strewn with the mangled corpses of friend and enemy, at the end of combat, we sense that Tolkien has himself witnessed that bleak devastation.

But in the main, Tolkien's imagination swerves away from Wilfred Owen's despair, mining the depths of his own sense of waste and loss, to salvage from it emotional, spiritual and moral meaning. This imaginative determination finds its way deep into the narrative fabric of his tales of Middle Earth.

In spite of the horror of total war, Tolkien chooses in his writing to focus his attention on the redemptive power of individual human action offered unconditionally as part of a common cause. Frodo Baggins is each of us aspiring to do good within modest limits: 'I should like to save the Shire, if I could,' says Frodo early on in his quest, 'though there have been times when I thought the inhabitants too stupid and dull for words.'

Tolkien's epic works are large-scale memorials to the modest struggles of ordinary people doing their best for good against the forces of inhumanity. They are a brilliantly achieved exemplar of the way the human imagination can configure a better future even in the aftermath of senseless, bloody destruction.

As such they sustain and offer solace. In 1940, Tolkien spoke of how 'to be caught in youth by 1914' was a 'hideous' experience. 'I was pitched into it all, just when I was full of stuff to write, and of things to learn; and never picked it all up again.' Yet his enduringly popular works – especially *The Hobbit* and *The Lord of the Rings* – have offered generations of readers the precious gift of an Ariadne's thread for their emotional yearnings, guiding them through the labyrinth of an ordinary life – giving it shape, giving it meaning, and above all, giving them hope.

preceding months had, Essex claimed, uncovered an elaborate plot, masterminded and financed by the Spanish government, to poison the Queen, restore the Catholic religion and seize the English throne. The would-be terrorist recruited to carry out the assassination, who had infiltrated the very Court itself, was none other than Dr Lopez.

Essex reported to the Queen in person that he had 'discovered a most dangerous and desperate treason'. The Queen remained unconvinced. Lopez, she insisted, was a trustworthy and loyal servant. Essex was a 'rash and temerarious youth', making claims he could not substantiate.

Nevertheless, Dr Lopez was held for 38 days without charge, before eventually being brought to trial. His home was subjected to a ruthlessly thorough search, ransacked and turned upside-down while his family stood by and watched. Nothing significant was uncovered. As one of Elizabeth's ministers reported to her: 'In the poor man's house were found no kind of writings of intelligences whereof he is accused.' Lopez was repeatedly interrogated, and eventually subjected to torture. On the rack, he confessed that he had accepted 50,000 crowns from the Spanish intelligence services to carry out the poisoning, using exotic drugs he had obtained abroad. He later retracted that confession.

Five years after the failed Spanish Armada, the English government remained in a state of agitation at the possibility of an imminent Catholic invasion from the European mainland. The country was still on high alert. Correspondence from overseas was regularly intercepted, dawn raids – carried out by the intelligence services – were normal. The public were told to be on the look-out for foreign spies and extremists in their midst, and to report suspicious individuals immediately. Personal freedom was curtailed in the interests of national security. The Elizabethan state had become, to all intents and purposes, a police state.

Dr Lopez was a Jewish immigrant, born in Portugal. He had studied medicine in Spain before settling in London in his thirties. There he quickly established himself as a successful society doctor, first at St Bartholomew's Hospital, and later as the personal physician to leading members of the English Government. He prospered, took an English wife, and settled in a comfortable city house. Lopez reached the pinnacle of his career when he was appointed personal physician to Queen Elizabeth herself.

At the end of February, 1594, Lopez was tried in camera, by a special commission at London's Guildhall, charged with leaking intelligence to the King of Spain, attempting to stir up rebellion, and conspiring to poison the Queen. Found guilty on all charges, he was hanged, drawn and quartered alongside two fellow alleged conspirators in June. Right to the end, Lopez protested his innocence.

In the fraught 1590s, not much was needed to convince a jittery public of the guilt of a foreigner, who dressed distinctively, and practised what seemed like an outlandish religion. The evidence used to convict Lopez had been obtained while he was under police surveillance. It consisted of an intercepted letter, sent to him by one of his so-called co-conspirators. This contained the sentence: 'This Bearer will tell you the price of your Pearls, and about a little Musk and Amber which I am determined to buy.'

According to the evidence of Essex's intelligence officers,

here was a coded set of instructions. 'This Bearer will tell you the price of your Pearls' meant that Lopez's offer to assassinate the Queen was accepted and he should carry it out forthwith. The 'Musk and Amber which [his correspondent was] determined to buy' meant that the King of Spain would then immediately attack and burn the Queen's fleet, anchored in the Thames. Ludicrous as this sounds to us today, in the atmosphere of terrorist-hunting hysteria which prevailed, the 'evidence' of the letter was accepted as conclusive proof of Lopez's guilt.

A new report from the influential Home Affairs Committee has concluded that the extension of the time limit for detention of terrorist suspects from 14 to 28 is justified, because of the amount of time police investigation of suspected terrorists takes. Indeed, the Committee's Chairman, John Denham MP, told the *Today* programme that 'If the current trends towards more conspiracies and more complex conspiracies continues, then we may well get to the point where 28 days isn't sufficient.'

Shortly before he made this observation, John Denham had also publicly defended the need for control orders to restrict the movement of suspected terrorists. Control orders, he said, are a 'justifiable safety valve' as 'proper protection of civil society'.

It was Michael Mansfield QC, responding to Denham's remarks, who made me think about the case of Dr Lopez. Mansfield cautioned us against using the argument that because we live in particularly perilous times we have to be prepared to give up 'due judicial process'. 'This is not a new problem,' he said. 'This is precisely the issue that infected

Elizabethan times. We have lived with plots, and spies and [allegations of conspiracies] for centuries.'

To give up 'due process' of the law is permanently to damage the personal freedom of each and every one of us. When we argue that detention arrangements and control orders must not infringe the human rights of an alleged perpetrator or suspect, we are not simply taking the 'liberal' point of view – we are also arguing for our own protection.

The Kahar brothers, arrested as terrorists during a dawn raid at Forest Gate in June 2006, on suspicion of preparing a chemical bomb, were eventually able to clear their names, and received a full police apology. In stark contrast, we will never know for sure whether the Portuguese physician, Dr Lopez, was innocent or guilty. He was held for more than a month with no clear idea of the reasons for his detention and was eventually tried in closed court session, without a legal representative present. He was denied the opportunity to counter the evidence against him, or to call witnesses.

In spite of his privileged position, entrusted with the health and welfare of the body of Queen Elizabeth I herself, Lopez's voice cannot be heard anywhere in the archival records, painstakingly preserved in the Elizabethan State Papers – he was silenced at the time, and remains so today. His voice is drowned out by the barrage of evidence systematically assembled against him by members of the security forces, convinced in advance of his guilt.

The processes of surveillance and information-gathering will always, as in the case of Dr Lopez and the Kahar brothers, be fallible. We ought each of us, then, to take their terrifying ordeals personally. However well-placed or well-connected we are, any one of us may some day find ourselves placed under suspicion, in need of the protection of the law against an accusation made unjustly or in error.

It was not until the end of the seventeenth century, by a slow process, during and after the English Civil Wars, that the civil liberties fatally undermined during the Age of Elizabeth began gradually to be restored. It took until the nineteenth century for the individual human rights we take for granted to become fully enshrined in law.

The process by which people who are alleged to have committed offences against the state are brought to court, so that the allegations against them can be properly examined, has been honed over centuries. Once dismantled, due process of the law will take centuries to rebuild.

If, in order to be able to detain those we suspect of intending harm, we reduce, for the time being, the long-established methods of accumulating evidence and establishing the burden of proof, how will we be able, at some future date, to reinstate them? How long will it take our children and our grandchildren to recognise the importance of what has been lost, to recover the rights we freely gave away?

Twelve

AND THEIR UNDERSTANDING THAT THE GOAL OF SCIENCE
WAS LIKELIHOOD RATHER THAN ABSOLUTE CERTAINTY,
A NUMBER OF LISTENERS WROTE TO ME TO OBJECT THAT
THERE HAD BEEN MANY CASES OF SCIENTISTS FAILING TO BE
SCRUPULOUS ABOUT THEIR FINDINGS, OR HAVING DOCTORED
THEIR RESULTS SO AS APPARENTLY TO PROVE A PARTICULAR
THEORY.

One of the biggest responses I have received from members
of the public in the course of my weekly 'Points of View'
came when I talked about experimental science – about the
way that science tries to arrive at the best fit between a general
principle and the laboratory evidence, but stops short of
claiming absolute certainty.

A number of people wrote reminding me that my description of scientists as men and women of integrity, painstakingly in pursuit of truth, did not quite tell the whole story. The pressure to be the first to reach a particular scientific goal has always been intense. The rewards in terms of personal fame and financial profit can be considerable. Consequently, some scientists have not been above falsifying the evidence in order to claim an important scientific 'breakthrough'.

There have been several notorious hoaxes in the history of science. In 1912, at a meeting of the Geological Society in London, Charles Dawson and Arthur Smith Woodward produced fragments of the skull of so-called Piltdown Man, allegedly discovered by workmen in gravel pits in Sussex. Dawson and Smith proposed that Piltdown man represented an evolutionary missing link between ape and man, and that it confirmed the current cutting-edge theory that a recognisably human brain developed early on in mankind's evolution.

Over forty years later, Piltdown Man was shown to be a composite forgery, put together by combining part of a medieval human skull, the 500-year-old lower jaw of an orang-utan, and chimpanzee fossil teeth. The deception went undetected for as long as it did because it provided the experts of the day with exactly what they wanted to support a considered scientific hypothesis. The fraudulent skull, with its sizeable brain cavity seemed to offer convincing evidence that human evolution was brain-led. Paleontologists were prepared to forgo normal scientific standards of scrutiny, because Piltdown man appeared to substantiate a theory they badly wanted to prove was correct.

Several of those who wrote to me, however, chose an example of a deception with graver consequences, that of Hwang Woo-suk, a pioneer of stem-cell research, once one of the world's most celebrated specialists in therapeutic cloning. Until recently he enjoyed celebrity status beyond that of any pop-star in his native South Korea, and his public appearances had all the razzmatazz of Hollywood. A postage stamp was even issued in his honour.

This month, 53-year-old Hwang has gone on trial, charged with deliberately falsifying his laboratory results and embezzling millions of pounds worth of state funding. He has already been disgraced, stripped of his honours and titles, and had his research licence revoked. If found guilty, he can expect a jail term of up to ten years.

Last summer Hwang and his team announced that they had created patient-specific stem-cell-derived tissue, based on cells taken from 11 separate people. Stem-cells are cells with the ability to develop into any type of tissue – say, tissue to replace a specific damaged organ. By inserting genetic material taken from a number of individual donors, Hwang's lab had for the first time used stem-cells to grow tissue which would match the exact genetic make-up of each one of them.

But six months later, an academic panel found that the results used to support Hwang's dramatic claim, published in the prestigious journal *Science*, had been 'intentionally fabricated'.

Photographs associated with the experiments had been doctored. Material from a single source had been adulterated so that it appeared to have come from separate donors. Here was something more serious than experimental error. Here was a 'hoax' or 'fraud' designed to take in the scientific establishment at the highest level.

Stem-cells could potentially be used to repair damaged or defective tissue anywhere in the body, such as the cells in the pancreas that stop producing insulin in diabetics, or the degenerating brain-cells in diseases such as Alzheimer's and Parkinson's – research like Hwang's could help millions of people worldwide. So the expectations on the part of doctors and patients, and the government and commercial pressures on scientists working in this field are enormous.

The pressure from the South Korean government – determined to be right at the forefront of technological and scientific innovation – for some dramatic pay-off was extreme. After promising initial experimental results, Hwang Woo-suk and his researchers succumbed to the temptation to fake key data so as to make the research outcomes appear more impressive than their findings justified.

One of the questions members of the scientific community are asking, is whether Hwang's deception could, or should have been discovered earlier. That question, inevitably, has been directed at *Science* magazine, which published the two papers announcing Hwang's supposedly landmark results.

It has brought into the public domain the process of 'peer review' – the method of assessment used within the academy to regulate and control research activity. In scientific research, that process is supposed to ensure that the methodology is sound, and that interpretation of data does not lead to misleading or unreasonable claims.

Peer review can have a beneficial damping effect on overeager practitioners – as one senior scientist comments, 'It is good at calming down over-optimistic claims.' But peer review is time-consuming – it involves reading the paper, producing detailed comments, evaluating its importance, and ranking it against others in the field. It is often inclined to err on the side of caution. Consensus tends to cohere around 'safe' projects, pushing just a little bit further the boundaries of already well-tried methods and outcomes, rather than supporting those which look more 'risky'.

No wonder work in new, sensitive fields like stem-cell research is increasingly being carried out in countries like China, where there is little or no regulation. In our world of instant communication and 24-hour news, a deliberative process like peer review can seem frustratingly slow. At the outer envelope of current laboratory research, perhaps the great leap forward might be in the direction indicated by the ambitious investigator, whose impatience to arrive first at the next great scientific milestone overcomes his or her proper experimental caution.

In 1885, Louis Pasteur demonstrated the effectiveness of his vaccine against rabies by inoculating a boy badly bitten by a rabid dog. It now emerges that Pasteur's public account of that experiment was carefully drafted to obscure the fact that it violated prevailing ethical standards for the conduct of human experiments – standards that Pasteur had himself just endorsed. Pasteur suggested that he had previously tested his vaccine on a 'large number' of dogs. In fact, his laboratory notebooks reveal that the patient was treated using a method that Pasteur had only recently decided to try, and that was entirely untested on animals. Had the truth come out at the time, Pasteur would probably have been disgraced. As it was, the vaccine's success was such that no doubts were ever raised.

Pasteur was a scientific gambler whose bet paid off. Gamblers try to force the pace of research, wagering that the experimental results they are currently fudging will come good. By the time the breakthrough has been properly made – a rabies vaccine, a cure for Parkinson's disease – they hope to have successfully produced the genuine evidence and to have achieved properly verifiable outcomes.

On the other hand, the scientific community pursues a policy of systematic self-regulating, making sure that the procedures followed are sound, and the data have not been exaggerated or manipulated. False claims, strenuously checked and tested, will eventually fail and be rejected. Sooner or later, Hwang's bogus stem-cell results would have come to light when they could not be replicated. The Piltdown man hoax was, in the end, uncovered, and the record set straight.

But financial incentives in the form of massive amounts of government funding are another matter. Political pressure from governments, pouring money directly into work in research areas they have set their hearts on leading, surely does have the capacity to distort even the best-established procedures.

What we must be watchful for are situations where the funding of science demands a rate of return on research invest-ment that increases intolerably the temptation to gamble. Might the blame for Hwang's deception lie, ultimately, at the feet of those who financed him so lavishly, and the state machine that over-inflated his reputation?

Thirteen

LIKE MANY BRITONS, I LOVE TO HOLIDAY IN PROVINCIAL
FRANCE, WHERE THE PACE OF LIFE IS SLOWER THAN AT HOME,
AS IS THE PACE OF CHANGE, AND A SHORT BREAK NEAR
MARSEILLE IN JULY 2006 PROVED A PARTICULARLY PLEASURABLE
ONE. BUT RESISTANCE TO CHANGE, I REALISED, HAS ITS DOWN-
SIDE. THE FRENCH HAVE SOMETIMES BEEN FAR SLOWER THAN
THE BRITISH TO RECOGNISE THE TALENT OF A NATIVE-BORN
ARTIST OF GENIUS.

I spent Bastille day with French friends in the beautiful fishing port of Cassis, sitting over a perfect meal of freshly-
grilled fish and rosé wine, on the sea-front, in the warm
evening air. We watched the celebration fireworks, as we have
done each year for almost 20 years, to the accompaniment,
over loudspeakers, of symphonic music, and the Mayor

reminding us that the 'ville de Cassis' had been following the same routine of fishing and cultivating its vines for 2000 years, since the Phocaeans founded nearby Marseille. Bouquets of silver and gold rockets burst into bloom high above us, exploding into armfuls of shimmering stars which filled the entire velvet-blue night sky.

Everything about the evening reinforced the pleasures that draw me to spend time in France whenever I can. Having arrived from London only hours earlier, I could practically feel the sense of well-being physically, on my skin, as a warmth and contentment induced by perfect, predictable pleasures. At my desk at home, the smell of grapes and pine-needles, the sound of the cicadas, the vibrant colours of the land-scape, are always available to dream about, always vivid to me – the more so because I can be so certain they will still be there when I arrive in the Midi.

The French refer to this (with, it seems to me, increasing insistence) as 'a quality of life'. Its components are: caring for a specific place; savouring the local cuisine (carefully adapted to suit the produce that grows in the locality); delight-ing in delicacies made and marketed in the 'quartier'; taking time to allow the familiar flavours to be savoured – rolled around the tongue. In other words, participating in all the traditions that make each particular corner of France unique.

And yes, there are the equally reliable annoyances too, that you can always count on – endearingly part of that French aversion not just to change, but to new rules which might interfere with long-enjoyed pleasures. In the modest brasserie where we ate steak and chips the following night, 'no smok-ing' notices were plastered all round the walls, but the locals cheerfully smoked their way through their meal – four cigarettes apiece per diner I calculated. And the steep cobbled streets of Cassis boasted the usual piles of dog-excrement, to booby-trap the passer-by in thongy sandals, in spite of signs threatening heavy penalties for 'fouling the pavement'.

Less reassuring was to share the concerns of our French friends about how their children would find the means to continue these traditions. Despite a good education and several hard-worked placements at very little money in Parisian financial institutions, there was now no guarantee of a job in their chosen profession, or any job at all. We love the fact that the man who serves us in our favourite café has done so for all the years we have been visiting – but where does that leave the youngster, straight out of school, looking for a job?

I found myself reflecting on the differences between the Anglo-Saxon and French temperaments. Our acceptance of inevitable and relentless change, the stress and continual pressure of work, followed by the rush home to further pressures and demands there, hoping all the while for some deferred, future gratification. The French belief that the daily process of living deserves to be enjoyed now, in the importance of savouring life to the full, whether you work in a café, as a teacher, or run a substantial business.

Could we – would it be possible – I mused, to blend the French respect for place and commitment to much-loved traditions of everyday life with the resilience and flexibility of the British economy which seems to offer Europe one of its routes to future prosperity?

When I asked one of my French friends in his sixties if he

believed change in France was, in the end, inevitable, he sighed, turned his glass of wine around lovingly in his hand, and said, 'I don't think the French will ever accept rapid change, it is not in our nature. We understand all too clearly the price we pay. Morale here is certainly low. But there are sacrifices we are just not prepared to make.' His twenty-five-year-old son was just as certain that things could not go on as they are. 'Eventually my girlfriend and I will leave France. London is the place to make one's way now.' His father looked visibly depressed.

Last April, student protests forced the French government to scrap a proposed new youth employment law which would have allowed employers to fire employees under the age of 26, at the end of a two-year contract. The young protesters argued that they were entitled to the same security of tenure as that enjoyed by their elders. But to our friend's son, a two-year contract seemed like a marvellous prospect, a chance to prove himself. I imagine the unemployed and marginalised young Muslims who rioted in the suburbs of Paris in the winter of 2005 would agree.

A few days later, as our long-weekend break drew to a close, I went to the 'Cézanne in Provence' exhibition at the Musée Granet in Aix-en-Provence, a breathtaking bringing together of over a hundred of Paul Cézanne's paintings for the anniversary of his death. In the shadow of the mountain of Sainte-Victoire – the mountain whose shifting shades and angles Cézanne spent a lifetime trying to recapitulate in paint – the whole region paid visible homage. Knots of people waited patiently for admission (the exhibition was booked days and sometimes weeks in advance). Every shop in the neighbourhood carried Cézanne memorabilia in its window.

Stepping from the blue, ochre and green of the sun-soaked Provence landscape into the cool, white air-conditioned interior of the museum was like entering a cathedral. There was a hush, a concentration, an aura of veneration. But whereas most cathedrals these days are sparsely populated, these soaring spaces were crowded, packed with people marvelling at the great artist's ability to capture forever the essence of Provence in what seem like a few, rapidly executed brush-strokes. Those standing spellbound in front of the works were from all over the world, and yet by far the majority of them were French – families, elderly couples, school-parties, young back-packers and tanned sun-worshippers.

Cézanne would have found all this hard to believe. It dawned on me slowly that the total lack of recognition for his talent, which he experienced in his home town of Aix-en-Provence during his entire lifetime was connected to that very French love of the familiar, and resistance to change that so seduce me whenever I visit.

Cézanne was born in Aix-en-Provence in 1839. By his early twenties he had abandoned the legal studies his banker father had insisted he embark on, and moved into the world of art encouraged by his childhood friend, the novelist Émile Zola (they later quarrelled, and ceased to speak to one another). During the 1870s Cézanne began to paint almost exclusively outdoors, producing vibrant 'plein-air' paintings in the manner which was coming to be called 'Impressionist'. Towards the end of his life, he resettled in Aix-en-Provence and produced the works for which he is best remembered –

richly textured and coloured landscapes in and around his home town, above all, view after view of his beloved mountain.

Every year, from 1863 onwards, Cézanne submitted his paintings to the jury of the Official Salon in Paris – France's official art showcase. With the exception of one portrait, in 1882, they were all rejected. The work of Impressionists like Cézanne simply broke too many of the rules, shattered too many much-loved French artistic conventions. During Cézanne's lifetime, the residents of Aix-en-Provence dismissed him as an untalented eccentric. The director of the Musée Granet swore that he would never allow his collection to be desecrated by his 'daubs'. The first Cézanne painting was exhibited there in 1953.

There must, surely, be some way to retain 'quality of life' in the midst of the kind of rapid change and economic success we in Britain currently enjoy. But if I have to choose, I know that I belong temperamentally in a culture which will be able to recognise, seize upon and celebrate immediately, with confidence, the next Paul Cézanne.

of school-work (I was always a bit of a blue-stocking), when I was grabbed hold of by three or four grey and faceless people. They put me into an oversized greatcoat, and enveloped my head in a headscarf, pulled firmly down over my forehead and knotted under my chin. I would wake in terror as I realised that I was no longer an A-stream English schoolgirl with a bright future. The scarf had turned me into a cipher, a nobody.

It's easy now to see what the contemporary events were that fuelled the anxiety in my dream in the early 1950s. My childhood was full of post-war images of seemingly interminable snaking lines of dispossessed people, people who had lost everything, the women bundled in ill-fitting garments with their hair shrouded, patiently waiting for bread, patiently waiting for visas. I don't recall that we were ever shown the queues of Jews waiting to be herded on to trains on their way to the gas-chambers – that was an awful secret our parents preferred not to reveal to us. But I do remember that as the child of Jewish immigrants, every time I saw a girl just like myself, in a hand-me-down coat and a headscarf, I knew with absolute certainty that that could easily have been me.

That dream of mine and the situation that produced it – the movements of peoples forced into homelessness by circumstances beyond their control – are now part of history. They belong to Europe's shared, defining memories of its twentieth-century past. For me, as an historian, the past is the place where we can focus without blinking on the feelings and attitudes of former times, as they connect with, and enable us to come to terms with, ideas less easily grasped in the present. History lets me see the here-and-now more clearly, to begin to understand and make better sense of the present. And so it turned out to be with my dream.

In the autumn of 1992, a pale young woman, her face barely visible behind a patterned scarf, and bundled in a man's duffel-coat, was ushered into my Head of Department's office in the University of London. She was from Sarajevo, and was working down the road from the college, cleaning offices. Could she perhaps sit in on some of our lectures and classes? Before the collapse of Old Yugoslavia she had been doing a degree in English Literature at the University of Sarajevo. Now, a refugee, worried sick about her family – the siege of Sarajevo was still going on, and she could get no word of them – she needed something that would connect her with her old life, something to give her new one meaning.

She handed me her documents. These, it turned out, contained not just her passport details, but also all her results from the three years of her degree course. She was a good student with consistently high grades; she would have graduated in the coming year.

As I leafed through her papers, a wave of shock broke over me. On page one of the booklet of official documents was her passport photo. It showed a bold, smiling young woman with shiny, bobbed black hair and pearl earrings. She wore a smart dark jacket over a scoop-necked jumper, and her mouth was a bright red cupid's bow. She was, in other words, exactly like any ambitious, able, confident young woman her age. The huddled figure in my office armchair was barely recognisable as the same person. Wearing that incongruous headscarf – a garment she would not have dreamed of donning in happier times – she had become a nobody, a lost soul. It was as if my dream had returned to haunt me, and was sitting in front of me.

Fortunately, we were able to do more for Sandra than simply let her sit in on classes. Her documented university record allowed us to admit her as a transfer student to the University of London. The following year she graduated with a good degree. Over the next three years, we helped other young women from Old Yugoslavia, who like her had walked out of a war zone under gunfire, and hitched rides across Europe to safety, to begin to build new lives for themselves. Several of them are now prominent figures in their own right.

My dream came back to me once again in a flash, as I watched the pictures on the television news of leading seaman Faye Turney, an experienced sea-survival specialist, and coxwain of the boat whose crew were seized by Iranian Republican Guards, wearing a scarf.

One minute, there Faye Turney had been, in naval uniform steering a small boat, on patrol in the waters that divide Iran from Iraq. The next thing we knew, she was dressed in shapeless garments and a headscarf, and appearing on television as a nobody, a vulnerable, defenceless little woman. Just as I had feared as a child, her competence and training became invisible, we could no longer see her for what she still was, even in captivity – a qualified person, doing a difficult job.

For days, even after the detainees' release, the British press were mesmerised by the charade of Faye Turney's television appearances. On one such occasion during the diplomatic stand-off between Britain and Iran, I woke to hear Colonel Bob Stewart, the first British UN commander in Bosnia in the early 1990s, being asked on the *Today* programme by Carolyn Quinn whether the detention of British marines and seamen by Iran had raised questions about whether women soldiers and sailors ought to be allowed to serve on the front line.

Colonel Stewart believed it had. 'People like myself are a little unsettled,' he responded. 'If that wasn't the case she wouldn't have been on the front page of all the newspapers for 12 days. So there is disquiet among a lot of people in this country that a woman has been put into this position.'

But what was making Colonel Stewart and the rest of us uneasy, surely, were feelings created out of the same stuff as my childhood nightmare. A piece of propaganda had proved shockingly effective with the British public. Simply by the way they had dressed her, a régime which insists that, for modesty's sake, women must cover their hair and their bodies at all times, had succeeded in making us begin to talk as though there was something intrinsically shameful about allowing women in our armed forces to serve on the front line.

Like so many of the rights gained by women over the past fifty years, those of women in the armed services have been hard won. Women now make up almost one in 10 of Britain's military personnel. Over three-quarters of all jobs in the armed forces are now open to women. Like my Sarajevan students, before calamity struck, Faye Turney believed that in her chosen career she was on an equal footing with the men serving alongside her. Interviewed by the BBC shortly before her detention about life on the edge of a war zone, she told us proudly that she'd wanted to join the armed forces 'ever since I was ten'. Like my displaced students she had found herself a helpless ghost through circumstances beyond her control.

The seizure of British naval personnel has turned out to be a tawdry episode for Britain and Iran – hijacked by propagandists on both sides, no-one, I believe, has come out of it looking good. But it may at least have reminded us how little it can still take, even in a country like our own, in which equality for men and women is a secure reality, to revive the ghosts of the past. It still, apparently, only takes a headscarf – just as I feared, all those years ago, at the age of ten, each time I woke in distress from my familiar bad dream.

Fifteen

A WEEKEND VISIT TO A STATELY HOME NEAR BATH COINCIDED WITH THE APPEARANCE OF AN ARTICLE BY THE CULTURE MINISTER ABOUT THE CRUCIAL PART 'HERITAGE' AND THE ARTS WERE TO PLAY IN THE 2012 OLYMPICS IN ADDING TO THE ENJOYMENT OF THE MANY OVERSEAS VISITORS WHO WOULD FLOCK TO BRITAIN FOR THE ATHLETICS. BUT MY VISIT TO DYRHAM PARK WAS A VIVID REMINDER OF THE FACT THAT UNDERSTANDING OUR HISTORIC CULTURE IS NOT JUST A MATTER OF A PLEASANT AFTERNOON OUT.

On a sunny spring weekend, Dyrham Park, just outside Bath, the stately home of William Blathwayt, is the perfect National Trust property to visit. It has everything the Secretary of State for Culture, Media and Sport hopes to promote to the world as 'heritage' for the 2012 Olympics.

As you round the final bend of the long driveway, the seventeenth-century house comes majestically into view, set in beautiful parkland with grazing fallow deer, beneath the spreading shade of centuries-old trees, its carefully-tended flower-beds studded with kaleidoscope-coloured tulips.

When I was last there, the honey-coloured stone of the handsome three-storey façade was bathed in golden light, and the adjoining Orangery with its double-height glass windows smelled of green shade, citrus and palms. Children romped on the rolling landscaped lawns. The house itself was a welcome respite from the bright light outside.

Inside, some three hundred years after the original owner's death, the surroundings are sumptuous – glorious walnut panelling and a sensational cedar and cypress staircase; gilded embossed-leather wall-coverings, inlaid furniture, tapestries and rugs. On the walls are fine Dutch landscapes and perspective paintings in a manner that was enormously fashionable at the end of the seventeenth century. And there are fantastic pieces of blue-and-white Delft faïence everywhere, including a pair of waist-high pagoda-like pyramid vases designed for the display of rare tulips – another expensive seventeenth century fad on which William Blathwayt was happy to spend a small fortune.

The house at Dyrham Park belonged to the family of Blathwayt's wife, Mary Wynter. Having met and married his heiress in his late thirties, Blathwayt set about transforming her Tudor manor house into a mansion in the latest fashionable style, with interior decoration to match.

So who was William Blathwayt? Frankly, he was a somewhat prosaic government official with expensive tastes.

Willliam III, whom he served with exceptional efficiency as Secretary of War, and Auditor General at the Colonial Office, pronounced him 'dull'. The diarist John Evelyn called him, 'a very proper person, and very dextrous in businesse' adding, 'and has besides all this married a very great fortune'. Old money looked down on him, pronouncing his expenditure on Dyrham Park excessive and unwisely spent: 'My Lord Scarborough thinks he lays out his money not very well'.

Where did all his money come from? Well, he was William and Mary's 'imperial fixer'. His successful career was based on the way he could make things happen, at long-distance, throughout English-administered territories, from its American colonies to its farthest-flung tropical island outposts. For this he was handsomely remunerated over a period of twenty-five years, between the 1680s and the turn of the century.

But Blathwayt's salary certainly did not stretch to cover his magnificent lifestyle at Dyrham Park. That was maintained by systematically extracting backhanders from his 'clients'.

If you want him to act, one of Blathwayt's agents advised the Governor of the Island of St Christopher in the Caribbean (now St Kitts), it will cost you: 'Without a gratification of twenty or thirty guineas for himself at least', he wrote, 'I much doubt the effect of anything else.' The Governor duly sent thirty guineas on behalf of the colony, and added another ten of his own with an accompanying note: 'To buy you a pair of gloves in acknowledgement of the favour you did me in my business at Court.'

This explains a great deal about that very grand house. The receiving rooms in Blathwayt's mansion are panelled in black walnut, courtesy of the Governor of Maryland. The cypress and cedar wood for the balluster and stair risers of the grand main staircase were a gift from the Governor of South Carolina, the walnut treads were the contribution of the Governor of Virginia. The juniper floorboards came from Jamaica. The extensive gardens, which once boasted some of the most impressive fountains and cascades in England, were planted with exotic foreign plants collected for Blathwayt by colonial officials engaged in business which needed his blessing.

Blathwayt did choose and purchase the Delft ware, the ornamental tiles and splendid Dutch pottery himself – as well as oriental silks and large quantities of tea – whenever he accompanied King William to The Hague on royal business. But he made sure that he was charged absolutely no customs duties on them – remonstrating indignantly with anybody who so much as tried.

On my recent visit to Dyrham Park I tried to keep Blathwayt's unscrupulous behaviour at the front of my mind. Here was beauty created out of selfishness, for the Blathwayt family's benefit alone. The National Trust had become its custodian only after the family's money finally ran out in the 20th century. Surely knowing this would take the edge off any pleasure I might take in all that opulence? It did not. In fact, it did quite the opposite. Remembering Blathwayt's ruthless acquisitiveness gave my visitor-experience a kind of tension and edginess. It made me think.

I have to admit that I consider that the act of wrestling with my conscience while enjoying a day out in the country is the proper way of engaging with the historic past. My guide-book, by contrast, seemed concerned to erase as far as possible all morally awkward aspects of the house and its former owner, and instead to stress the 'tranquil, but fragile, spirit of Dyrham'.

Too much of what we are offered in the way of publicly funded art now has to be designed to be enjoyed with the minimum of effort. The 'quality of the visit' and 'visitor satisfaction' have become the measures of an attraction's success (and a condition of future funding). So nothing must trouble our tour of the gallery or trip to the ballet.

Under pressure to please, our arts funding organisations risk becoming spoon-feeders of our leisure-time. Just sit back and enjoy. Re-branded as 'heritage', our day-trips to spectacular sites of beauty, visits to national museums, the opera and the ballet, become merely spectator sports. The 2012 Olympic Games will be just like our arts experiences – pleasant ways to spend a day out. This conveniently allows the DCMS to run the claims to government financial support of the 'heritage industries' and the 'legacy games' seamlessly together.

How else could Tessa Jowell, writing about the involvement in the arts in the forthcoming Olympics in the *Observer*, have confidently suggested that 2012 would be a golden 'Olympic opportunity', which 'the cultural sector is better placed than ever to take advantage of'? She went on to claim that diverting 5 per cent of Arts Council funding into sport for four years, starting in 2009, is something anyone interested in the arts ought to applaud.

William Blathwayt's profligate getting and spending on art and architecture had none of the worthy aims the DCMS insists on attaching to the nation's historical and current cultural collections. Most of our great art collections and our stately homes were originally assembled by entrepreneurs, exuberantly indulging their personal tastes and pleasures. They have come down to us largely by historical accident, as gifts to the nation – often prompted by the need to offset death duties.

In 2003, for example, two Dutch flower-paintings, which Blathwayt would have given a great deal to have had hanging in his panelled reception rooms, were accepted as 'cultural treasures' in lieu of inheritance tax by the DCMS. One of them, an exquisitely detailed painting by Balthasar van der Ast, of a bouquet of exotic flowers in a pewter jug on a ledge, with a grasshopper and fallen petals, is on view at the National Gallery in London. The other, by Roeland Savery, has a lizard and a dragonfly alongside the lovingly painted flower arrangement. It now hangs in Cambridge's Fitzwilliam Museum.

Perhaps, then, instead of wringing our hands at the continual erosion of government grants and dwindling support from the Lottery, we in the arts community should turn our attention elsewhere. Those who have accumulated enormous fortunes – the less-unscrupulous William Blathwayts of today – have also built themselves magnificent homes and assembled collections of carefully chosen art works. We need to make sure that they too will eventually make that cultural heritage available to the nation as a whole.

Which means lobbying the Treasury for much better tax breaks on substantial gifts to the nation, and more generous and imaginative acceptance of 'cultural treasures' in lieu of death duties. The cost to the government of financial incentives for giving will be considerable. But some of us are beginning to think that strategies like these for securing our future cultural heritage are preferable to over-administered public sector handouts.

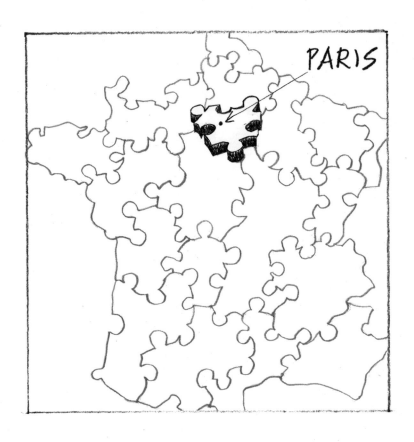

PARIS

Sixteen

HALFWAY THROUGH THE FRENCH PRESIDENTIAL ELECTION CAMPAIGN IN APRIL 2007, DURING THE CAMPAIGNING WHICH PRECEDED THE RUN-OFF BETWEEN RIGHT-WING CANDIDATE NICOLAS SARKOZY AND SOCIALIST SEGOLENE ROYAL, I FOUND MYSELF CONCERNED AT THE WAY MEDIA COVERAGE OF THE TWO CANDIDATES ON THE CAMPAIGN TRAIL WAS ALMOST EXCLUSIVELY FOCUSED ON PARIS, IN SPITE OF FRANCE'S EXTRAORDINARY REGIONAL DIVERSITY. THAT LED ME ON TO REFLECT ON THE CLEVER WAY IN WHICH THE FRENCH HAVE MANAGED TO RETAIN THE DISTINCTIVENESS OF LOCAL PRODUCE AND CUSTOMS.

It is sometimes easy to forget just how big France is. It is by far the largest country in the European Union – bigger than Spain, and twice the size of the UK. And despite its network of motorways, it will take you two days to drive comfortably from its northernmost border at the English Channel to its sun-drenched southern coast, lapped by the Mediterranean.

The pictures on the television news showing revellers celebrating the conservative Nicolas Sarkozy and socialist Segolene Royal's success in making the second round of the presidential election, were almost entirely focused on Paris. They gave us no hint of the significantly different reactions of communities away from the capital. They barely addressed the fact that France is a country of distinctive local cultures, richly varied, and fiercely independent of one another.

Perhaps on account of its size, France led Europe in producing scientifically measured maps. At the beginning of the 1670s, the French king, Louis XIV, invited the renowned Italian astronomer Giovanni Domenico Cassini to take charge of his new Royal Observatory, just outside Paris. Between 1676 and 1681, a team of French astronomers, using Cassini's new method for determining longitude, based on tables of observations of the moons of Jupiter, mapped France's entire coastline, and established the exact dimensions of Louis XIV's kingdom.

Cassini's new map of France was published in 1693, its new contours directly superimposed on an outline of the best previous map. The town of Brest on Brittany's westernmost point could be seen to have moved a full fifty miles eastwards, and the redrafting showed dramatically that France had been reduced in size by a fifth. The king was allegedly prompted to remark that he had lost more land to his astronomers than his enemies had ever taken from him in battle.

If you have ever travelled by road across France, it is

practically certain that you will have been tempted at least once to take a turn off your route, to follow an intriguing signpost pointing to the region's 'musée locale' – the museum devoted to whatever that region is most famous for. Every wine-producing region will, of course, have its museum of 'vines and wine-making'. At Camembert, Saint Marcelin and Livarot there will be a Museum of Cheese devoted to the history of its local manufacture, the utensils used in the process, and the scientific stages of fermentation.

Grasse, 'cradle of traditional perfume making', naturally boasts a Perfume Museum. One of the regional museums dearest to my own heart is at Ménerbes in the Luberon – the Museum of the Cork-Screw, dedicated to that essential piece of equipment associated with the wine industry. It boasts a thousand individual, hand-crafted cork-screws, the oldest dating from the end of the seventeenth century. In Aquitaine, not far from Bordeaux, is the complementary Museum of the Wine-bottle Cork, where you can follow the manufacturing process which begins with the stripping of bark from the cork oak trees.

As I'm an oyster-lover, though, my favourite local museum is the Museum of the Oyster in the fishing-village of Bouzigues, not far from Montpellier. Here you can learn how seed-oysters are attached to vertical hemp ropes strung on wooden frames, running vertically down to the sea bed. There they grow until the ropes are hauled up and the mature oysters harvested. Every aspect of the life of the 'peasants of the sea' – the oyster fishermen – is lovingly recreated, and you can follow your visit with a boat tour around the oyster beds themselves. At the end of my last visit, I bought a pewter-cast pair of oyster shells, forming a charming container, which sits on a shelf in my kitchen, and in which I keep sea salt from nearby Aigues-Mortes (which naturally boasts its own Museum of Salt).

Museums like these are born out of French local pride in the traditional activities which have shaped their 'terroir' – giving each locality its typical landscape and buildings, and sustaining the lives of its population, close to the earth. This is the same proud temperament that currently makes France so resistant to change. Rapid change, the French will assure you, will produce homogeneity, and lead to the erasure of those special local qualities that have always sustained them.

The rhetoric of both candidates embarking on the second round of the French presidential election is aimed at reassuring the electorate that necessary change will not come at too high a price. And yet, in their hearts, the French must know that the days are over when any government could justify subsidising smallholder-produced, richly-varied market produce, and supporting small local specialist manufacturers with special tax-exemptions. There is a hollow ring, these days, to the mantra, that 'quality of life is worth sustaining at any cost'.

Those in France who fear that new economic measures introduced by either Sarkozy or Royal are bound to destroy a much-loved way of life, might, however, take comfort from us here in Britain. Here, drastic economic reforms have given rise to a prosperous, confident nation. And gradually, the regionality which we too cherished and believed threatened, is coming back – in viable form. My example of such a successful revival, it may not surprise you to hear, is the oyster industry at Whitstable.

The Romans were the first visitors to discover the wonders of the Whitstable oyster – an extremely local delicacy, which thrived on the particular environment and sea-bed formation off the Kent cost. A flourishing economy developed along-side the oysters – a profitable fishing-fleet, harvesting and grading factories, and a wide variety of eateries. In the 1850s the Whitstable Company of Free Fishers and Dredgers sent 80 million oysters to Billingsgate a year. Abundant oysters became the fast-food fad of the nineteenth century, on sale for just a few pence a dozen.

By the twentieth century, demand had fallen, and, follow-ing three exceptionally severe winters (when the sea froze over, right across to the Isle of Sheppey), and disastrous floods in 1953, the oyster beds came to the brink of extinction.

But in the 1990s, under modern management and using new technologies for breeding and hatching the seed-oysters, the Whitstable Oyster Fishery Company brought the indus-try back to life. In 2002, Whitstable oyster beds once again produced a harvest of 'Whitstable natives' – locally raised, quality oysters – for the London market. Today Whitstable is once more a thriving village, thronged with visitors and DFLs – 'Down From Londoners' as the locals call us – eagerly demolishing plate-loads of delicious oysters, as well as clams, lobsters, and freshly-caught fish, washed down with locally-brewed Whitstable beer.

I am not being overly dewy-eyed. This is not the same clien-tele that used to come down by charabanc to the seaside, to end a day paddling in the chilly sea with a paper of fish and chips, or a bag of fresh oysters. It is now the professional classes who choose to spend the weekend in Whitstable, and the hotel prices reflect the change. But the distinctiveness is back, and the local economy is thriving, and – unlike Herne Bay and Margate down the coast – young people have come back to live and work.

On my last visit there, I walked on the beach at Whitstable with my husband as dusk fell, enjoying the beauty of the sea and looking forward to a dozen of those Whitstable natives – appreciating the local 'terroir', just as the French have always done.

And indeed, if we look a little closer at those charming local museums dotted across France, we notice that the regional products they celebrate also came close to disappearing at the beginning of the last century. The cork oak trees on which Aquitaine's wine-bottle cork-manufacture depended were wiped out by a combination of natural disasters in the 1850s, giving way to the distinctive maritime pines we now associate with the French coast. They turned instead to imported Spanish cork, introduced new techniques and machinery, and production once again flourished. And oyster-production at Bouzigues, just as at Whitstable, almost came to an end around 1900 – until 'new technology' was introduced by enterprising local fishermen, in the form of today's wooden frames with their suspended ropes of oysters, nurtured and harvested using modern methods and machinery.

So the French, it turns out, already know how to adapt regional manufacture to altered circumstances and how to embrace the market. They simply need the courage to believe that treasured ways of life will survive the transition from the old ways to the new, whatever the new French Presidency brings in the way of economic change.

Seventeen

WE NO LONGER BELIEVE, AS WAS WIDELY HELD IN THE 1580S, THAT A SMALL EARTHQUAKE IN BRITAIN IS A SIGN OF GOD'S DIVINE WRATH, DIRECTED AGAINST HIS WAYWARD PEOPLE. WE DO, HOWEVER, SEEM INCLINED TO BEHAVE AS IF CLIMATE CHANGES WHICH ARE SYMPTOMATIC OF GLOBAL WARNING WERE BEYOND OUR POWER TO BEGIN TO REVERSE AND RECTIFY.

We live in a world of immediate, global news. We are used to turning on the radio to a report that a natural disaster has struck in some far away part of the world – a major earthquake has occurred in San Francisco, Los Angeles or Mexico City, along the San Andreas fault; a tsunami threatens Indonesia, where four tectonic plates jostle one another off the coast of Sumatra. Last Saturday morning's report of a sizeable earthquake which had rocked parts of Kent, damaging buildings and disrupting electricity supplies, was alarmingly closer to home. It was not, however, an unheard of event for the south of England.

At 6 o'clock on the evening of 6 April 1580, Gabriel Harvey – the self-important Cambridge Professor of Rhetoric, and friend of poet Edmund Spenser – was at the home of a gentleman friend in Essex, playing cards. Without warning, everything around them began to rattle and pulsate:

'The earth under us quaked,' he reported, 'and the house shaked above; besides the moving and rattling of the table and forms [benches] where we sat.'

Concentrating as he was on the rather good hand he had been dealt, Harvey claims at first to have thought the effect was caused by noisy footsteps in an upstairs room. His host, however, soon came 'stumbling into the Parlour, somewhat strangely affrighted, and in a manner all aghast', to tell them that he and all his servants had experienced a violent motion of the entire building. Sending out to the nearest town, he had been informed that an earthquake had indeed taken place, causing extensive damage.

The ladies present professed themselves 'never so scared in their life'. 'I beseech you heartily,' said one of them, 'let us leave off playing, and fall a praying.' Gabriel Harvey would have none of it. In characteristically professorial fashion, he proceeded to sit the household down and give them a stern lecture on how there was always a rational explanation for alarming natural phenomena. He denounced the superstitious riff-raff who saw in every violent storm, comet, eclipse or earthquake a divine portent of some punishment about to befall the human race. He argued (at some length) that although the earthquake was clearly an act of God, it could still be explained in purely natural terms. And although his science was limited, he made a stab at explaining the 'exhalations of wind' from beneath the earth's surface, which had given rise to it.

The flood of pamphlets published in London in the weeks that followed were, however, much less circumspect. Boasting lurid, attention-grabbing titles, they warned that the earthquake was a sign from God that the end of the world was at hand: 'A bright burning beacon forewarning all wise virgins to trim their lamps against the coming of the Bridegroom'; 'A discourse of the end of this world: And a prayer for the appeasing of God's wrath and indignation'.

In a pamphlet catchily entitled, 'A warning for the wise, a feare to the fond, a bridle to the lewd, and a glass to the good' – Thomas Churchyard included a poem he had written, urging the citizens of London to prepare for the Last Judgment:

An Earthquake came, with whirling noise as House and Tower should fall:
A loving rod of threatening wrath, sent sure to warn us all.

The earthquake of April 1580 seems to have been the largest in the recorded history of seismic activity in England (modern estimates put it at 5½ on the Richter scale). Its epicentre was in the Dover Straits, and the damage it inflicted stretched from London to France and Flanders.

At Dover itself, a piece of the cliffs fell, and so did part of the castle wall. About half a dozen chimney stacks came down in London, and a pinnacle about a foot in length toppled off Westminster Abbey. Terrified playgoers at the Curtain Theatre in Hollywell had to jump from the playhouse balconies, since 'they could no way shift for themselves, unless they would, by leaping, hazard their lives or limbs'.

A passenger on a boat from Dover reported that the vessel on which he was travelling had touched the sea bed five times and that the ensuing waves had risen well above the ship's mast. Twelve hours later, a tidal wave struck the coast at Dover, demolishing houses, and pulverising ships along the shore.

Contemporary accounts are as vivid as any tabloid newspaper's today: 'It chanced also, Thomas Cobhed being in the pulpit in Christ's church in Newgate market, preaching to the people, suddenly the church so shook, that out of the roof of the same fell certain great stones, by the fall whereof, a boy named Thomas Gray, apprentice to John Spurling Shoemaker, was brained, and Mabel Everet his fellow servant, was stricken on the head with a stone, being dangerously hurt, but is not dead: and a number of the people (by hasting to flee and escape away) were sore bruised and hurt, by falls and such like accidents.'

More than four hundred years later, eyewitness accounts of an earthquake off Folkestone, in May 2007, read remarkably similarly:

Carpenter Terry Croker, 30, was in bed when the tremor began. 'Everything was quiet when all of a sudden, the walls started to vibrate,' he recalls. 'Then I heard this massive rumble, and all this soot and rubble started to pour out of the chimney into the fireplace in our room. I couldn't work out what on earth was going on.'

No-one, however, as far as I am aware, has suggested that Folkestone's earthquake was a warning that the end of the world is at hand. We no longer treat earthquakes (or indeed the appearance of a bright comet in the night sky) as auguries of Armageddon – wake-up calls to humanity to correct their wayward behaviour before it is too late. Scientific explanation has freed us from the bonds of superstition where such natural phenomena are concerned. Evidence painstakingly assembled by observation, over more than a century, not only allows seismologists to understand – and explain to us – precisely how earthquakes happen, but also to anticipate likely future occurrences.

Neither precise measurement nor confident predictions of precise outcomes seem to be available, however, when it comes to the natural disaster the general public is most preoccupied with today – global warming.

For weeks, in the spring of 2007, the press seemed to take a perverse delight in warning us that this had been the warmest April since records began, more than three hundred years ago. 'The Met Office said that temperatures during the first half of the month had been consistently two or three degrees above average, and often much more. Already temperatures in London have reached 80F (26.5C)', trumpeted the *Telegraph*.

The media response to this April surge in temperature statistics was a predictable clamour of concern about climate change. 'This is the latest in a series of statistics to bolster claims that global warming is in full swing', the *Mirror* told its readers.

I hope that nobody is any longer in any doubt that global warming is a real phenomenon, and that – possibly for the first time in history – its likely calamitous consequences are of mankind's own making. But I don't personally find the tone or content of the newspaper articles helpful. 'What', I want to know, 'am I supposed to do about it?' Am I allowed to enjoy the good weather, or must I retreat in alarm into my study to await the knell of doom?

These are rhetorical questions, of course. But while we are increasingly offered any number of lurid figures and tabulated statistics about how bad things have got, I find it difficult to locate correspondingly clear tables to tell me what would constitute an effective response on my own part. If I were to decide to enjoy the sunshine at home, and cancel all family holiday trips by plane, how many trips, by how many families, would it take to arrest the quickening pace of warming?

Some of these figures are, of course available. What bothers me is the fact that they are rarely ever there on the page alongside the prophecies of doom. As long as this is the case, in my view, we are being barely more responsible than Gabriel Harvey's card-playing partners, rushing screaming to the top of the house to fall on their knees, in the hope of avoiding the wrath of the Almighty. If we are going to make responsible judgments, scientifically, we need the data laid clearly before us, so that we can decide together, rationally and responsibly, how to begin to redress the damage.

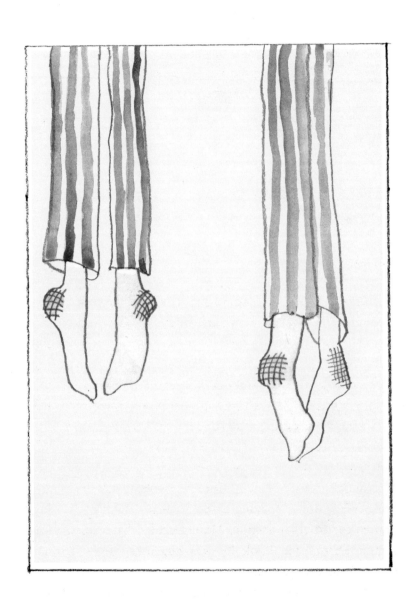

Eighteen

I CONFESS THAT THE PIECE THAT FOLLOWS IS ONE OF MY
FAVOURITE 'POINTS OF VIEW' TO DATE. IT CAME ABOUT AS A
RESULT OF A REAL EXCHANGE WITH MY SON ON THE SUBJECT
OF DARNING, AND DEVELOPED INTO A SERIES OF DISCUSSIONS
BETWEEN HIM AND MYSELF ABOUT TRUMAN CAPOTE'S *IN COLD
BLOOD* (WHICH I HAD NOT READ FOR MANY YEARS, BUT WAS
PROMPTED TO REREAD) AND THE FILM *CAPOTE* (WHICH ON HIS
RECOMMENDATION I WENT TO SEE).

My youngest son looked up from his book, to ask me a question. 'What does "darning a sock" mean?' Puzzled, I asked him to repeat the question. He responded by reading me a sentence from the book he was engrossed in – Truman Capote's *In Cold Blood*:

"'Later that same evening, another woman, in another

kitchen, put aside a sock she was darning, [and] removed a pair of plastic-rimmed spectacles".

'What does "darning a sock" mean?'

Vivid images flashed before my eyes. Myself in lovat-green uniform in the first year of secondary school, a wooden darning mushroom tucked inside an old school games sock, darning-needle poised. The terrifying Miss Kennard barking instructions at the class, as if we were taking part in a military campaign, telling us how to create the meticulous pattern of running-stitches and interwoven threads that would turn the hole in the heel into a gratifyingly neat lattice of wool. The genuine satisfaction of having been frugal – having made the sock 'as good as new', for another season's wear.

When did I stop darning? I think it must have been in the early 1980s, probably when we gave up woollen socks in favour of something synthetic, or cotton mix. I don't believe I was darning any longer by the time my son was born in 1984, any more than I was mending three-cornered tears, or fixing the ladders in pairs of stockings.

'Do you really mean you don't know?' I asked, incredu-lously. He really didn't. Nor, when I explained, could he quite understand the point. Perfectly adequate socks were on sale in packs of 3 or more pairs, in every supermarket. Why would you bother to mend a sock when you could simply buy a new pair?

There is a touch of enchantment for me about the idea that an active verb could fall out of recognition because the activity it describes seems no longer to serve a purpose. It says so much about the power of language to capture our lived experience. As long as a word can conjure up a vivid picture in our minds it maintains a fingertip-hold on the collective imagination. Once those pictures are irretrievably lost, so is the word's ability to convey meaning richly to us – significance derived from shared experience, beneath the surface of the words themselves.

But to get back to darning. The fact that my exchange with my son should have taken place over a book like Truman Capote's *In Cold Blood* set me thinking. An absolutely pioneering piece of writing, Capote called it the first 'non-fiction novel'. It is avowedly a work of literature – the fruit of Capote's exceptional insights and imagination – in which the facts have been so painstakingly and meticulously researched and assembled that it is almost impossible not to think of it as in the strictest sense, true.

In Cold Blood tells the story of the motiveless, mindless murder of the unbearably ordinary Clutter family, in the small town of Holcomb in Kansas, in the early hours of 15 November 1959 (Herb Clutter, his wife Bonnie, sixteen-year-old Nancy and fifteen-year-old Kenyon). The most shocking thing about the tale is the absolute senselessness of the atrocity. The family were prosperous but not rich; they were God-fearing members of the local community; they were well-liked, and had done nobody any harm that anyone could fathom. The murderers were two damaged and abused misfits, thrown together in prison, to which they had been committed for pathetically minor offences. The villains crossed paths with the victims through a mixture of bad luck and faulty information.

Capote's book was first published in 1965. So compelling is its documentary account of the way appalling acts of violence are the outcome of accidental concatenations of events, that I have always thought of it as a parable for all time. Capote's closely observed portrait of Perry Smith, the intelligent, narcissistic fantasist who allegedly carried out all four of the murders, continues to stand as a convincing portrait of a recurrent type of deluded killer incapable of remorse.

The more I reflected, the more 'darning' seemed to represent a good many other things in the story of the everyday lives of the murderers and their victims, as told by Capote, which were sufficiently unlike our own times that it ought to give us pause for thought. The day-dream scenarios and fantasies of celebrity Perry Smith recorded in his notebooks were drawn from the newspapers, or sensationalist Hollywood movies. There were no computers or computer games, no internet or chat-rooms. The carnage he and Dick Hickock caused was carried out with a knife and a shotgun – neither man had access to the automatic and semi-automatic weapons readily available to today's pettiest criminals.

By sheer coincidence, my son and I were having our discussion of *In Cold Blood* just as news broke of the chillingly carefully pre-meditated murder, at Blacksburg, Virginia, of 32 randomly selected Virginia Tech University students and teachers by Korean fellow-student Seung-Hui Cho. Like the close-knit community of residents of Holcomb, Kansas, we all – residents in the global village which is today's news information network – were stunned by the senselessness of the crime, and randomness of the slaughter.

There were, chillingly, shared features in the delusional

fantasies of the perpetrators of the two atrocities, in spite of the separation in time. Like Perry Smith in his notebooks, Seung-Hui Cho represented himself in his private, self-aggrandising rantings as a spurned outsider, whose talents had been cruelly trampled upon by those around him, and as a crucified Christ-figure, rejected and humiliated. Like Smith, the Virginia Tech assassin also dramatised himself as potentially a celebrity and super-hero – modelling himself on the gun-brandishing protagonists in violent movies and computer games. Both had planned their outrage meticulously, buying specialist equipment for its successful completion for weeks before the event itself. Neither at any stage showed any sign of contrition or compassion.

Still there are obvious differences. The world Perry Smith inhabited was a world in which darning was a familiar part of the scenery. Darning crops up again in *In Cold Blood* as one of the compassionate domestic services the undersheriff of Garden City, Kansas's wife, Mrs Meier, performs for the inmates in the jail: 'she cooks and sews for the prisoners, darns, does their laundry'. Perry's cell was actually inside the living quarters of the undersheriff and his family (in order to keep him separate from his accomplice), and Capote has Mrs Meier preparing his favourite meal of Spanish rice for him – reaching out to him, even though her husband warns her that if she had been one of the first on the scene of the Clutter killings as he had, she would have been less forgiving.

Such traditional community ways of connecting were apparently not there at the beginning of the twenty-first century for Seung-Hui Cho. Instead, like many modern loners, he found his communities online, in cyberspace. Rather than forging – however falteringly – the communal bonds that hold isolated individuals precariously within the network of shared human lives, Cho's virtual encounters exacerbated and amplified his paranoid behaviour.

What, however, struck me most, when – prompted by my son's question – I returned to *In Cold Blood*, was how starkly it showed that the close community and traditional values of Holcomb, Kansas were no protection whatsoever against a random act of extreme violence which took place in their midst. They offered no defence against the chance encounter between the Clutters and two damaged petty drifters with nothing to lose.

There are those who look back to consolingly close, homogeneous communities like Holcomb, and call them better times. I do not share that view. But I do think we need to look long and hard at the nature of the ties that bind us one to the other today.

We have come a long way since the small-town prejudices and bigotries of the 50s and 60s. New, largely uncharted, ever-more global communities make increasingly strong claims on our lives, over our immediate surroundings. More of us are obliged to look at our lived experience in less narrowly focused ways than before. And this increases the need for us actively to build the flexible communities in which we find ourselves, with infinite care. Because in our global village, chance encounters will happen increasingly frequently, and so will the potential for disastrous misunderstanding and mindless violence. We have a responsibility to make our new world more comfortable than the old.

We cannot afford to wait, nostalgically recalling a world in which we, the fortunate ones, the insiders, sat around the family hearth in our cosy world, compassionately darning socks for those we had failed to include.

Nineteen

ALTHOUGH ALBERT EINSTEIN IS AN ICONIC FIGURE IN THE
PUBLIC IMAGINATION – THE EPITOME OF A BRILLIANT SCIENTIST
– NOT EVERYONE KNOWS THAT HE SPENT SEVERAL EXTENDED
PERIODS CARRYING OUT HIS GROUNDBREAKING RESEARCH IN
CALIFORNIA, WHERE HE FELL IN LOVE WITH HOLLYWOOD. A
VISIT TO CALTECH IN PASADENA, WHERE EINSTEIN HAD WORKED
IN THE EARLY 1930S, IN LATE SPRING 2007, REMINDED ME OF
THE HISTORICALLY STRONG SET OF VALUES SHARED BY BRITAIN
AND THE UNITED STATES WHICH HAS CONTRIBUTED IMPOR-
TANTLY TO POST-WAR SCIENCE AND SCIENTIFIC RESPONSIBILITY.

The campus of the California Institute of Technology –
Caltech – in Pasadena looks more like a Latin-American
hacienda than a top-flight university dedicated to teaching
and research in fundamental science.

Practically all the giants of modern science have been associated with Caltech during the hundred years since its foundation. The best known of these by far is Albert Einstein, perhaps science's only folk hero – Nobel-Prize-winning theoretical physicist, forever associated with the evocative formula $E = mc^2$. Caltech is where Linus Pauling pursued his research on the formation of chemical bonds between atoms in molecules and crystals, paving the way for Crick and Watson's discovery of the structure of DNA. This is also where Edwin Hubble's discoveries with the Mount Wilson telescope challenged Einstein's cosmological picture of the universe, and brought him here himself to discuss the implications of his general theory of relativity with Caltech physicists and astronomers.

The Institute sits at the foot of the San Gabriel Mountains, in a lush landscape. When I was there recently, graceful jacaranda trees smothered in a purple haze of blossom, and soaring emerald-leaved palms, shaded beds of bird-of-paradise flowers and headily-scented star jasmine. A long avenue of mature olive trees runs through the sunlit campus, to a pool on whose edge dozens of ebony-coloured turtles sun themselves among the reeds. Arched colonnades covered in bougainvillaea border and connect the cool stuccoed buildings.

Walk up close, though, and these buildings have unexpectedly futuristic names: the Keith Spalding Building, home of the Space Infrared Telescope Facility; the Lauritsen Laboratory for high energy physics; and, a few short miles away, the Jet Propulsion Laboratory and its current project LISA – the laser interferometer space antenna. In this highly-charged intellectual environment, 2,000 undergraduate and graduate students, and 300 faculty work at the cutting edge of modern science.

Einstein visited Caltech for the first time in December 1930, returning in 1931–2 and 1932–3. It was while he was on his third research visit that the Nazis came to power in Germany. Einstein never returned to Europe, although he would spend the last twenty years of his life at the Institute for Advanced Study in Princeton rather than Caltech.

And it is here at Caltech that the formidable project of transcribing and publishing the entire Einstein archive is currently being carried out. Tucked into a corner of the Caltech campus is a modest building which contains the Einstein Papers Project. Housed deep in its basement, in a row of locked black filing cabinets running the full length of one wall, are copies of more than 70,000 items – half a million pages of documentation – relating to Einstein's life and career (most originals are kept at the Hebrew University of Jerusalem, to which Einstein bequeathed them at his death in 1955).

Einstein's devoted assistant Helen Dukas began collecting and ordering Einstein's papers in Berlin, even before he left for America. The collection includes Einstein's letters, scientific manuscripts (published and unpublished), as well as lectures, speeches and articles on a wide range of topics from the philosophy of science to education, Zionism, pacifism, and civil liberties. At Caltech a small team of dedicated researchers are editing the entire contents of the archive, transcribing them, annotating them, and publishing them volume by volume. I was given a guided tour, and shown some of the fascinating items the collection contains.

Among the papers are personal travel diaries Einstein kept whenever he was abroad. The diaries for the Caltech years give a wonderfully vivid picture of the élan with which he embraced his new California lifestyle. By the 30s Einstein was an international celebrity – the *Los Angeles Times* and the *Pasadena Star* newspapers produced over 1200 articles about him, which are also carefully filed in the Einstein archive. From the day he arrived he was fêted and honoured.

He loved Hollywood, and Hollywood loved him. On his first trip a motion picture tycoon made arrangements for Einstein and his wife Elsa to see his new film at the Universal studios. In his diary Einstein wrote: 'We drove to Hollywood to visit the film giant Laemmle. They showed us All Quiet on the Western Front, a nice piece, which the Nazis have banned successfully in Germany.' That ban, he also noted, was 'a diplomatic defeat for [the German] government'. Hearing that Einstein admired the films of Charlie Chaplin, Chaplin himself invited the couple to dinner, together with the newspaper magnate Randolph Hearst. Mary Pickford and Douglas Fairbanks entertained the Einsteins at their mansion, 'Pickfair', in Beverley Hills. It was, Einstein tells us, like a three-ringed circus, but he loved it nonetheless.

Of course, the Einstein papers for the Caltech years are full of important science too. But the very human Einstein who emerges from the pages of the California travel diaries is for me a kind of symbol for the way in which the United States took up the torch of fundamental scientific research and kept its flame alight, giving great original thinkers like Einstein a home and public recognition, when National Socialism in Germany was turning its back on the future.

It is also, for me, a reminder that the ties that bind European intellectuals to our fellow human beings in the United States are far stronger than the political agendas of particular political administrations on either side of the Atlantic. If we take the long view – back to the founding years of Caltech, and forward, beyond the disaster of the Iraq war, and what some like myself regard as the damagingly anti-science ethos of the Bush administration – the common intellectual understanding between our two countries has to continue to be nurtured and cherished.

Beneath the surface differences in attitudes and beliefs, there runs an historically strong set of values connecting us. It was out of the debris of World War Two, and the teamwork and collaboration between leading scientists in America and Europe that one of the lastingly important statements about war and weapons of mass destruction was issued by a group of distinguished scientists which included a number of Caltech *illuminati* – the 'Russell-Einstein manifesto'.

Together, Einstein in America and Bertrand Russell in England produced what still stands as one of the most important manifestos for the need for cooperation between nations. It was the last letter Einstein signed, shortly before he died on 18 April 1955, having drafted and redrafted the text with Russell in the weeks before his death.

The Russell-Einstein manifesto was addressed to the leaders of the western world. It urged them to recognise that weapons of war (specifically the atomic bomb) were now too deadly for war between opposed factions any longer to be an option:

'In the tragic situation which confronts humanity [they wrote], we feel that scientists should assemble in conference to appraise the perils that have arisen as a result of the development of weapons of mass destruction . . .

We have to learn to think in a new way [they went on]. We have to learn to ask ourselves, not what steps can be taken to give military victory to whatever group we prefer, for there no longer are such steps; the question we have to ask ourselves is: what steps can be taken to prevent a military contest of which the issue must be disastrous to all parties?'

The current clamour of anti-American sentiment in Europe runs entirely counter to Einstein and Russell's fervent hopes for the future. Just as they feared, it drives the world towards shrill factionalism and petty nationalistic posturing. But our response cannot be to deny the bonds of history and common aspiration which underpin decades of shared intellectual activities in Europe and America. We should not treat the Anglo-American accord as a doctrine to be imposed elsewhere in the world by military might, but rather redouble our efforts to build on our remarkable shared history of scientific advance.

As I wandered the campus at Caltech on my most recent visit, and as I talked to faculty and students, the culture of serious reflection on the big issues in science and in human values filled me with a sense that together they and we could achieve a great deal for the future of the human race. As my plane touched down back at Heathrow on my return, it struck me forcibly that we must hold on to that strong sense I had at Caltech of future purpose and possibility. We must not squander science's dream of an increasingly open world of discovery and opportunity.

the original

Twenty

IN THE LAST FULL WEEK IN MAY 2007, I WOKE EARLY ON THE MONDAY MORNING WITH THE THOUGHT UPPERMOST IN MY MIND THAT I HAD YET TO FIND A SUBJECT FOR THAT WEEK'S *A POINT OF VIEW*. TURNING ON THE RADIO I WAS AGHAST TO HEAR THAT THE *CUTTY SARK* WAS ABLAZE IN ITS DRY-DOCK IN GREENWICH. BY THE FOLLOWING DAY WE KNEW THAT THE HULL WAS BEYOND RESCUE APART FROM ITS FRAME, ALTHOUGH, FORTUNATELY, PRECIOUS FITTINGS HAD BEEN REMOVED TO SAFE-KEEPING DURING RENOVATION. MY TALK THAT WEEK WAS, I THINK, ESPECIALLY PASSIONATE, AND ALSO SUCCEEDED IN POSING A PHILOSOPHICAL QUESTION WHICH MANY LISTENERS FOUND FASCINATING.

I have spoken more than once, in the course of these broadcasts, of my fascination as an historian with the survival of things from the past, and the way touching and handling objects, or fragments of material, can help us recall with particular vividness and intensity otherwise inaccessible moments in history.

So listeners will not be surprised to hear that the news to which I woke on Monday morning – that the nineteenth-century tea-clipper, the *Cutty Sark* was ablaze from end to end at Greenwich – filled me with absolute dismay. Currently undergoing a £25 million restoration, the *Cutty Sark* is the kind of magnet draw for the general public which convinces them (to use the slogan cleverly coined last year) that 'History Matters'. One of London's most familiar landmarks since it was towed to its specially constructed dry dock in 1954, this much-loved ship is also a memorial to the merchant seamen who lost their lives at sea during two world wars. Since the *Cutty Sark* opened as a tourist attraction in 1957, millions of people have queued to tour it, or have participated in one of the many educational events on board.

By Tuesday morning, when the TV cameras were allowed closer, it was clear that the damage was extensive. The ship's three wooden decks and planking had been destroyed, and the intensity of the heat had in some places buckled the metal frame. Dramatic shots through the blackened hull showed that the ship had been reduced to a charred skeleton.

Still, it could, we were reassured, have been much worse. Because of the restoration in progress, half of the ship's timbers had been taken away for treatment. The three, 100-foot masts, their sails and rigging, had been removed at the beginning of the project and sent to Chatham's Historic Dockyard for storage. The prow, anchor and ship's wheel, and the complete contents of the below-decks galley and workshops, were also safe, as was the distinctive figurehead. This (many listeners will recall) features a busty 'witch' in a short petticoat allegedly called in Scots dialect a 'cutty sark'. Her hair flies backwards in the wind, and she holds aloft a horse's tail made of old rope.

And although 'everyone involved in the project is devastated', according to a statement from the *Cutty Sark* Trust's Chief Executive, still, here too was a golden opportunity, the possibility of restoring the ship to an even more stunning standard than had been envisaged before the tragedy.

I was almost persuaded that the fire had been a help rather than a hindrance to the restoration project. Part of our national heritage had come close to annihilation, but, fortunately (to quote the Chief Executive again, surveying the damage on Tuesday morning), 'we have enough of the original material here to make sure she will survive'.

I find this an interesting thought. Whatever happens now – and surely the restoration efforts will be redoubled, and the desperately needed extra funding forthcoming – the resulting ship will now conclusively be a 'replica', not the original.

But then, wasn't it that already? The masts, everything on deck, many of the deck planks, and the fittings, were remade from scratch the last time the ship was rescued from destruction (this time by decay and neglect) in the 1950s. The masts, sails and rigging were once again restored, and pieces of the fabric replaced, as part of the celebrations for the Millennium.

Some cultures seem to mind less than others whether the historical object has remained the same over time. The first time I visited Japan, I was struck by the contrast between the way the Japanese view their historic buildings, and the way we do ours. In Japan, where wooden buildings have always been terribly vulnerable to the ravages of earthquake and fire, the idea that something is in effect a 'replica' does not carry the same stigma of the inauthentic.

On our first morning in Osaka, we opened the curtains of our hotel room to discover that our attentive host had booked us a room with a 'royal' view of Osaka Castle. The five-storey green and white, pagoda-like building rose magnificently above the surrounding trees, its soaring copper roofs, outlined and ornamented with a filigree of gold, shimmering through the early-morning haze, dominating the sky-line.

Osaka Castle was completed around 1590 by the great military ruler of Osaka, Toyotomi Hideyoshi, and is today part of a proud heritage for the residents of Osaka and Japan.

Yet this beloved historical landmark is entirely a reproduction. Razed to the ground for the first time in 1615, ravaged by an explosion and fire in 1665, burned to the ground again when it was captured in 1868, heavily bombed in 1945, Osaka Castle was completely rebuilt as a concrete structure in 1932, and its exterior restored to its present splendour in the late 1990s. As our guide-book boasted: 'there remains no single piece of stone wall from the Toyotomi period.'

Later in our trip we took a bus from Kyoto to Kiyomizu-dera (the Clear Water Temple), which, like the *Cutty Sark* and Maritime Greenwich, is a UNESCO-designated World Heritage Site. The origins of Kiyomizu-dera can be traced back to 798 AD, when a priest from nearby Nara was instructed by a vision to construct a Buddhist shrine there on an existing Shinto sacred site. Today you climb two dauntingly long flights of steps (it was hot and humid the day we were there), and eventually arrive at the Main Hall, roofed in cypress, in front of which is a breathtakingly-cantilevered wooden platform, which projects out thirty feet, dizzyingly, over forty-foot cliffs, giving an unforgettable view of the forested landscape below. Descending another flight of steep steps to the secluded valley nestled beneath the main buildings, you find the 'clear water' of the temple's name, dropping vertically as a waterfall, and queue to stand beneath it, drinking the supposedly-therapeutic waters from a cup on a long wooden pole, which you dip into the sacred pool.

Yet here again, the present buildings are nowhere near as old as the history of the shrine suggests. Some of them date from the seventeenth century, others have been substantially restored in the 1980s. This last restoration included repainting the exterior of the soaring three-storey pagoda its original bright reddish-orange. Once again, this causes the Japanese no hint of anxiety – our guide-book informed us proudly that 'the main temple has been destroyed and rebuilt many times in its centuries of history'.

In Europe, by contrast, we have a tendency to disparage or overlook the history of objects that have failed to last, or survive only as 'replicas', 'reproductions' or 'recreations'. Holbein's paintings, produced for the court of King Henry VIII in the early decades of the sixteenth century, receive an enormous amount of attention from art historians and the public alike – as the numbers attending the 'Holbein in England' exhibition at Tate Britain at the end of last year confirmed. King Henry himself, however, was far less interested in panel paintings than in his fabulous collection of

5,000 tapestries – more time-consuming and expensive to make, more valuable and highly coveted by other European royals, and much more impressive when hung. Most of his tapestries, however, failed to survive the damp English climate – unlike Philip II's fabulous collection of sixteenth-century tapestries, still in the Prado in Madrid. So tapestries are, on the whole, neglected in discussions of Tudor court culture.

Following the fire, I may need to learn a more Japanese historical state of mind when it comes to the *Cutty Sark*. The shock of seeing that charred hull makes even a historical purist like myself welcome the prospect of resurrecting her as a glamorous 'replica'. Perhaps 'facsimile' would be a better way of describing her – made similar to the original.

At what point, indeed, in the replacement of almost every damaged element in the ship – including, perhaps, now, parts of the buckled frame – does it cease to be the 'original'? It comes down to that old philosophical conundrum, known as 'Is this my grandfather's axe?' My father replaced the blade of the axe, and I replace its handle. So is it still my grand-father's axe?

The original Greek version of this philosophical problem of identity and persistence, known as 'the ship of Theseus' is particularly apposite here. In his *Life of Theseus*, Plutarch tells us that the Athenians preserved and revered the ship in which Theseus returned from Crete, after he had rescued Ariadne from the Minotaur. Over time, however, they assid-uously replaced rotten planks with new timber, until every plank of the ship had eventually been replaced. So is this still Theseus's ship?

art lover

Twenty-one

THE ARCHITECT COLIN ST JOHN WILSON (KNOWN THROUGH-
OUT HIS LIFE AS SANDY) DIED ON 14 MAY 2007. ON 25 MAY
THE LAST BUILDING HE DESIGNED, PALLANT HOUSE GALLERY
IN CHICHESTER, WON THE PRESTIGIOUS GULBENKIAN PRIZE.
MONDAY OF THAT WEEK WAS A BANK HOLIDAY, AND I TOOK
ADVANTAGE OF IT TO TRAVEL TO CHICHESTER IN THE POUR-
ING RAIN TO PAY HOMAGE TO ONE OF THE GREATS OF MODERN
BRITISH ARCHITECTURE. WHAT I DID NOT APPRECIATE UNTIL
I GOT THERE WAS THAT SANDY WILSON HAD ALSO BEEN A
CONSIDERABLE COLLECTOR OF CONTEMPORARY BRITISH ART.

Ever since it first opened in 1998, I have been an admirer of
the new British Library building at St Pancras, designed by
Sir Colin St John Wilson, who died this month. It is hard
now to remember the controversy the library caused – the

chorus of indignant disapproval from those who maintained that its sleek, stepped-back red-brick buildings were inappropriate for a national landmark. Or who preferred the hopelessly slow service and uncomfortable environment of the old round reading room at the British Museum, to the speedy, automated delivery of books from its vast underground book stacks, and the sumptuously appointed, light and airy reading spaces on the Euston Road.

So when the new Pallant House Gallery in Chichester, the last building designed by Sandy Wilson (as he was always known), won the 2007 Gulbenkian Prize for the best new development in a UK museum or gallery, I decided to take advantage of the Bank Holiday to visit it.

Rounding the corner of Pallant Street in the rain, we got our first glimpse of the new wing adjoining the Grade 1-listed Queen Anne town house which used to house the whole collection. The juxtaposition of old and new is instantly sympathetic. Here is Sandy Wilson's trademark red brick – itself a deliberate reference to the work of Finnish architect Alvar Aalto he so admired – echoing the brick of the original house, echoing indeed the British Library, but on a more intimate scale. Where it joins the house, the discreet façade of the new building is faced in rich brown, salt-glazed terracotta tiling, tiling which also ornaments the recessed glass and steel entrance. Decorative incisions run vertically upwards suggesting glimpses of the interior, but the frontage otherwise encloses rather than discloses.

Once inside, the spacious foyer is a light, airy surprise. Wrapping around an inner garden courtyard, the nine gallery spaces are classic pure-white, top-lit rooms floored in light oak. A startlingly strong collection of modern painting by key British artists is displayed in a lofty upper gallery, flanked by domestic-sized spaces that perfectly suit the scale of the works. But the inviting interior is not the only surprise the gallery holds. Once inside, I found myself convincingly in the presence of a collection of twentieth-century British paintings and sculpture as thoughtfully selected and compelling as the building itself, and which represents Sandy Wilson's lifelong love-affair with twentieth century art.

For Wilson was not only the architect here, he was also a major benefactor, whose gift of more than 400 works from his extraordinary personal collection of contemporary art was the catalyst for the new gallery extension. That collection tells an important story about a tradition in British art which is all-too-easily overlooked alongside the razzmatazz of more recent high-profile millionaire collectors and badly-behaved, attention-seeking Young British Artists.

Sandy Wilson began collecting art in the early 1950s, with a band of colleagues and friends – artists, designers and architects – most of them part of the Independent Group (a group of young creatives at the newly-formed Institute of Contemporary Arts to whose discussions of contemporary art and its meaning he was an enthusiastic contributor). They included the artists Richard Hamilton, Eduardo Paolozzi, Peter Blake and R. B. Kitaj. He has described how he began by acquiring single works – occasionally by purchase (his first painting was bought with his £35 demobilisation pay from the Navy in 1945), but more often, particularly at the beginning, by a kind of barter with friends for works he had fallen in love with.

On one occasion he turned out his pockets and offered Eduardo Paolozzi their contents, in exchange for a single piece ('it amounted to 37 shillings and 6 pence' he recalled). On another, Richard Hamilton parted with a proof of his screen print 'Adonis in Y-fronts' in exchange for a small sum 'to help cover the cost of printing'.

Each time Sandy Wilson fell in love with a work, the passion to acquire it was so powerful he characterised it as an addiction: 'Only a fellow addict can understand the catch in the breath and the thumping heart of love-at-first-sight that signals the next ("absolute must") acquisition', he wrote in 1999. Later he would agonise over what work or works he was prepared to 'part with', in order to buy something new he could not do without.

Over the years Sandy Wilson's collection grew and developed, until it became the extraordinary record of a generation we can browse and reflect on today at Pallant House. There is a strong sense of communality and shared purpose about it, just as there is a coherent timeframe, particularly concentrated on the 1950s through to the end of the 60s. As I moved among the paintings and occasional sculptures, it felt like eavesdropping on a conversation – a set of exchanges among individuals struggling with the bleak economic outlook and the associated muted, emotional austerity of the British post-war period.

In fact, after an afternoon spent among the twentieth-century figurative paintings by artists like Frank Auerbach and Lucien Freud, 'pop' artists like Peter Blake and Patrick Caulfield, ground-breaking prints, and the stunning series of screen-printed posters by Kitaj currently on exhibit from the

1960s, I came away steeped in the suppressed passions of post-war Britain, and with a stronger understanding of the journey Wilson, his contemporaries and successors, had taken in architecture from the post-war years, down to the end of the century.

Sandy Wilson's art collecting began, as did his career as an architect, around the time of the Festival of Britain in 1951, and its associated building projects – above all the iconic building of London's South Bank, the Festival Hall. Indeed, his first architectural job was in the office of Sir Leslie Martin, the Festival Hall's architect. Laying the foundation stone for the Festival Hall in 1949, the then prime minister Clement Attlee predicted that the exhibition and its festivities would pass into history, but that the concert hall would remain, and around it would rise 'buildings worthy to take their place with the best of old London and form part of the replanned London of the future'.

Yet for almost fifty years, while Sandy Wilson's artist friends exuberantly experimented with new ideas and futuristic forms, English public opinion generally set its face firmly against modern architecture. Architects attempting to innovate either with design or materials were pilloried – we need only recall the famous 'carbuncle' jibe by the Prince of Wales at the design for the National Gallery extension in Trafalgar Square, or Sandy Wilson's own 'thirty year war' over the British Library.

While the 'Wilson gift' at Pallant House Gallery proclaims its owner's visionary eye for art and design, it is also a lasting reminder that the young architects of the 1950s in Britain were impatient to build for the future, given half a chance.

Their dream was squandered in post-war intolerance of the unfamiliar, and cheap, quick-fix solutions to problems of function and form. Only fairly recently has there been a resurgence in more confident and considered modern buildings in Britain.

The message that densely layered buildings like the Pallant House Gallery and the British Library convey is that carefully made creative work takes time to conceive, time to refine and time to be thoughtfully executed. In 1995 Sandy Wilson described a successful building of this kind as one 'that has prospered in use over a number of years and still has the power to excite the mind and touch the heart'.

We can, as it happens, test out that idea that where the architectural process behind a building has been intense, we will over time come to love and cherish it.

This summer, the Royal Festival Hall reopens after two years of restoration and redevelopment. The occasion will be celebrated with an 'Overture weekend' – 48 hours of free, continuous performance, in which every part of the site will become a platform for world-class artists, artists in residence, resident orchestras, and amateur and professional choirs from around Britain.

Since 1951, London has indeed learned to love the Royal Festival Hall. I'd like to think that with its Gala reopening we will be celebrating more than just the building itself. We will also be celebrating the humanity and optimism of a generation of architects and artists – many of them directly inspired by Sandy Wilson – who came together in those critical post-war years, and whose work has been underappreciated for so long.

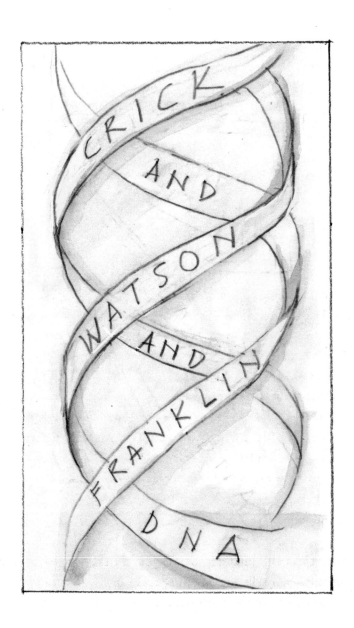

Twenty-two

THE GREAT NOBEL-PRIZE-WINNING SCIENTIST FRANCIS CRICK
DIED IN 2004. ON THE ANNIVERSARY OF HIS BIRTHDAY, I
CHOSE TO TALK ABOUT THE FURORE THAT HAD ACCOMPA-
NIED THE PUBLICATION OF HIS COLLABORATOR JAMES
WATSON'S COLOURFUL BOOK-LENGTH ACCOUNT OF THEIR
DISCOVERY, AND TO THINK ABOUT THE FACT THAT THOSE IN
THE PUBLIC EYE WOULD ALL LIKE TO BE ABLE TO RECORD
THEIR OWN ACCOUNTS OF THEIR LIFETIME ACHIEVEMENTS
FOR POSTERITY, BUT THAT IT WILL BE THE CONSIDERED
NARRATIVE OF HISTORY WHICH DECIDES THEIR SUCCESSES
AND FAILURES.

June 8th is the birthday of Francis Crick, who is lastingly
remembered for discovering the structure of DNA in 1953. That
set biologists on the path towards the secrets of the genetic

code, leading eventually to the human genome project, whose goal is to decipher the meaning of the billions of units of genetic information, unlocking cures for previously untreatable diseases.

So this is a good time to remember how the dramatic story of that scientific breakthrough first came to be told, and to think about the way such stories shape our collective memory of important moments in history – something Tony Blair might do well to consider.

In 1968 a scandal erupted at Harvard University. There was a rumour that Harvard University Press was refusing to publish *The Double Helix* – the inside story of the race to discover the structure of DNA. The book's author was James Watson, Crick's Cambridge collaborator, who had won the Nobel Prize for this brilliant breakthrough with Crick and Maurice Wilkins in 1962.

According to the *New York Times*: 'The university halted plans for publication when the two men who shared the Nobel Prize with Dr. Watson for this work, voiced protests.'

Crick and Wilkins were apparently objecting to parts of Watson's manuscript, because of derogatory remarks it made about several scientists involved. Publication, however, eventually went ahead. Watson removed the offending passages – though not those concerning Wilkins's collaborator, Rosalind Franklin, who had died of cancer in 1958.

Franklin's premature death had already prevented her sharing in the Nobel Prize (it is never awarded posthumously). Now she could not respond to Watson's disparaging remarks about her. Watson did later add an 'epilogue' in which he admitted that he had been wrong in some of his less flattering early impressions of Franklin. *The Double Helix* went on to become a bestseller.

At issue in the attempt to stop publication of Watson's book was the account he gave of the way ground-breaking scientific discoveries are made. Where the scientist had traditionally been presented as a white-coated, omniscient sage, Watson painted Crick and himself as film-stars – carpet-bagging adventurers and intellectual mischief-makers, spurred on by their desire to win at all costs. 'I have never seen Francis Crick in a modest mood', are the book's opening words.

Watson's *The Double Helix* is a colourful, partisan narrative account of the everyday lives of research scientists, and the complicated ways in which they move from routine laboratory work towards solving a problem identified as of major scientific importance. It is a thriller – full of accidents, remarks overheard and data stumbled upon by chance. There are brash remarks, rash promises, mistakes hastily withdrawn and reworked, personality clashes which hinder progress, and finally, glittering prizes for a few.

By the 1950s a number of molecular biologists had focused their attention on DNA as the likely carrier of human genetic material. The young James Watson first saw an X-ray diffraction photograph of the DNA molecule in 1951, while working as a post-doctoral student in a Copenhagen laboratory. He recognised that if genes were like crystals – as the detail of the photographs seemed to show – there was a possibility of discovering their fundamental structure using crystallography. He immediately switched his research to the Cavendish Laboratory in England, where Max Perutz was known to be working on the minute structure of large biological molecules.

Once there, Watson tells us, 'I knew I would not leave Cambridge for a long time. Departing would be idiocy, for I had discovered the fun of talking to Francis Crick.' Crick was a dashing figure – as voluble and excitable as Watson was gawky and shy. He also had a genuinely original mind. As Watson puts it: 'Francis's brain was a genuine asset.'

Crick was someone with the capacity to connect information gathered and processed from a wide range of sources and disciplines. He was full of ideas, impatient and easily bored, and loved nothing more than to engage with a similarly indefatigable antagonist in heated scientific debate. Watson became Crick's regular coffee-break companion in the laboratory, and they met increasingly often socially, where they continued their scientific discussions – when not distracted by their other shared obsession, the opposite sex.

What is remarkable is the speed with which, once Crick and Watson had identified the crux of the problem of DNA's structure, they managed to solve it. It was, scientists will tell you, exactly the right moment to do so – the key technology and vital techniques were available. In California, Linus Pauling had discovered that the basic structure of the protein molecule – a long chain molecule closely related to DNA – was helix-shaped. His unconventional technique for arriving at this conclusion involved a combination of guesswork and physical model-building. Crick and Watson decided to adopt the same strategy.

They played around with models made out of bits of a children's construction set, and they consulted Wilkins and

Franklin in London about their X-ray diffraction photographs (carefully concealing the reason for their interest).

A quarrel with Rosalind Franklin gave them their final, vital piece of data. On a visit to her lab, Watson, with typical brashness, lectured Franklin on the need for her to learn some theory, to interpret her photos of DNA. She exploded with anger, and he fled. In the safety of Wilkins's laboratory the two men moaned about working with difficult women, and Wilkins produced Rosalind Franklin's most recent X-ray diffraction photograph.

Watson tells us how he saw immediately that it told him what he needed to know:

'My mouth fell open and my pulse began to race. The pattern was unbelievably simpler than those obtained previously. It could arise only from a helical structure.'

He rushed back to Cambridge, with a sketch of the photo scribbled on the edge of his newspaper. In two months he and Crick had produced their double helix for scrutiny by the scientific community. Its simplicity was utterly convincing. A letter to the journal *Nature* announced the discovery with wonderful understatement:

'We wish to suggest a structure for the salt of deoxyribose nucleic acid (DNA). This structure has novel features which are of considerable biological interest.'

That is the story as Watson still likes to tell it – the beguiling tale people like myself cherish as a 'true life' scientific adventure story. Crick always saw it otherwise. In his view, their breakthrough was 'partly a matter of luck, and partly good judgement, inspiration and persistent application'.

The textbook account of the impact of the discovery is

different, too. In 2003, celebrating the 50th anniversary of the discovery, one commentator wrote in *Nature*: 'We usually think that the double-helix model acquired immediate and enduring success. On the contrary, it enjoyed only a quiet debut.' The arresting image of the double helix itself achieved iconic status, but Crick and Watson's breakthrough went largely unnoticed for a number of years.

'It was like a tree falling in the middle of the forest. It had no impact,' a distinguished scientist who was studying DNA in America at the time recalled. 'Most places just ignored it,' he said. 'Only history will tell whether Crick and Watson's contribution was a great leap forward, or one small step along the way.'

A reminder, then, for Tony Blair who last week travelled around Africa on a carefully choreographed farewell tour. At each of his stopping points he was showered with honours and praise in front of the world's media.

South African President Thabo Mbeki thanked the outgoing British prime minister for raising the plight of Africa on the world stage. He said he had been 'inspired' by the strong lead Blair had taken on behalf of the African people. 'We needed a very strong voice of support,' he said. 'Now there isn't anyone in the world who wouldn't think of putting the African issue on the agenda. Thanks a lot prime minister.'

I have no doubt at all that James Watson and Francis Crick were scientists of towering stature and brilliance. As an historian I understand the importance of narrative to give shape to the tide of events. But none of us is in a position, in the end, to tell our own story for posterity. Like Watson's *Double Helix*, Tony Blair's tale of well-judged interventions and courageous stands makes a ripping good yarn. But his personal faith in the difference he has made on the world stage will, in the end, have to stand the test of time, and the scrutiny of historians.

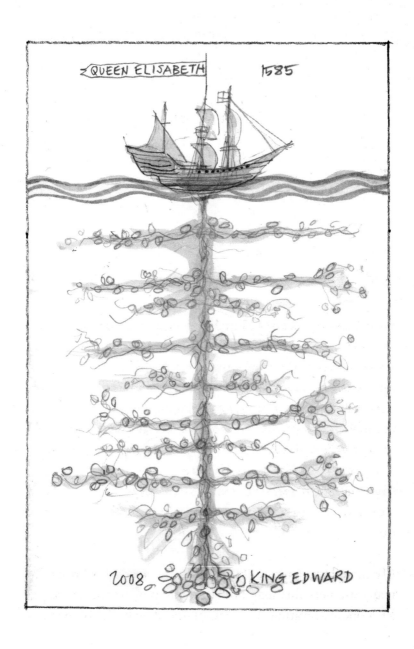

Twenty-three

TO BE HONEST, I WROTE ABOUT MY ATTEMPT TO GROW VEGETA-
BLES IN THE SMALL ROOF-GARDEN I AND MY HUSBAND HAVE
MANAGED TO CREATE OUTSIDE THE SIXTH FLOOR WINDOWS OF
OUR MANSION BLOCK FLAT, BECAUSE I WAS SO GENUINELY
DELIGHTED TO HAVE BEEN REASONABLY SUCCESSFUL IN PROD-
UCING RESPECTABLE CROPS OF POTATOES, TOMATOES AND BEANS
IN SO UNPROMISING AN ENVIRONMENT. I DISCOVERED THAT I
HAD STRUCK A CHORD WITH A NUMBER OF URBAN LISTENERS,
SOME OF WHOM EMAILED AND WROTE TO TELL ME OF THEIR
OWN UNUSUAL FRUITS AND VEGETABLES RAISED AGAINST THE
ODDS.

My first crop of new potatoes is almost ready for lifting. To
many listeners this may not seem an event worth recording,
let alone celebrating. But one of the drawbacks of being a

city-dweller is not having a garden. Instead I have a piece of roof, about the size of a rather large tablecloth, on which I do my best to live out my fantasy of being self-sufficient in home-grown vegetables. As I plant out my seedlings, or encourage my bean plants to wind themselves around their supporting frame, I have the sustaining sense of connecting back to my childhood and my family history, and of taking pleasure in knowing how to care for my own little bit of earth.

My potatoes (like my tomatoes) are in large non-matching earthenware containers, on a small terrace among the chimney-pots. When I clamber out to water them, the cool touch and fresh smell of their emerald green foliage fills me with satisfaction, and buoys up my spirits, before I plunge into the Underground for the first of several journeys of the day. I'd like to be able to tell you my little roof-garden was an urban Eden, but I can't pretend I give it enough attention for it truly to thrive.

Potatoes and tomatoes are something of a horticultural paradox. They both belong to the *solanaceae* family, a distinction they share with the nightshades, including deadly nightshade or belladonna. The tempting, deep blue-black berries of belladonna are fatal if eaten, and yet the similarity between its foliage, flowers and fruits, and those of two of the most widely cultivated vegetables in the world is strikingly close.

Today, according to the National Center for Food and Agricultural Policy in Washington, more than 110 million tonnes of tomatoes are produced annually worldwide, with four southern European countries – Greece, Italy, Portugal and Spain – together contributing 15 million tonnes. Two-thirds of all the tomatoes grown are for processing (for everything from tinned tomatoes to ketchup). The potato is now the fourth most important world food crop (after wheat, rice, and maize). In both cases, the cultivation and consumption of an indigenous South American plant, first described by European explorers in the sixteenth century, has gradually spread, to every continent except Antarctica, and strains have been developed which flourish and produce ample crops in an astonishing variety of climates and types of soil.

The culinary conquest of the world by the potato and tomato did not, however, happen overnight. In the early days of domestic cultivation of the tomato, people found it strange and disturbing that its flowers and foliage closely resembled those of a plant which if consumed caused a painful death. Although Europeans – especially Italians – were eating tomatoes raw and including them cooked in recipes by the eighteenth century, Americans had to be convinced that they would not be poisoned by them, as late as the nineteenth. A certain Robert Johnson, about whom nothing at all else is known, supposedly achieved a degree of celebrity, when he ate a tomato publicly on the steps of the courthouse in Salem, New Jersey in 1820, to prove it would do him no harm.

The potato was first identified as worth growing for its food value in Europe by sixteenth-century Spanish explorers, who found it under cultivation in Peru, Bolivia, Colombia, and Ecuador. They compared the unfamiliar tuber food crop to truffles, and treated them with comparable respect. The earliest specimens probably reached Spain around 1570, and, like the tomato, were initially mainly used medicinally, in small quantities, as an ingredient in pills, salves and thera-peutic potions. From Spain, the potato spread to Italy, the

Low Countries, and the British Isles – the story of the national disaster caused in Ireland by the repeated failure of the potato crop in the 1850s, is, of course, legendary.

The most plausible (though still probably apocryphal) story of the introduction of the potato into Europe attributes its 'discovery' to Sir Francis Drake. In 1585 he led a fleet of some 2 dozen ships on a piratical expedition to seize and loot the Spanish possessions in the West Indies, bent on bringing back cargo-loads of gold for Queen Elizabeth. Having plundered, pillaged and burned his way around the islands, he returned to England a year later with no treasure, but with a cargo of booty which included potato tubers and tobacco.

The sixteenth-century botanist John Gerard produced the first lifelike picture of the potato plant, depicting leaves, flowers, and tubers in his 1597 *Herball* (revised and made even more botanically accurate in the later edition of 1633). The potato plant appears to have held a particular fascination for him, since he is depicted in the *Herball*'s frontispiece illustration, holding a flowering sprig of the potato plant.

All of which makes it clear that one of the attractive characteristics of the potato is that it is easy to grow – it thrives almost anywhere, and even the most modestly talented gardener can produce a successful crop.

This is just as well in my own case, since as far as I am aware, nobody ever taught me how to garden. When my husband asked me curiously how I knew how to prick out my beetroot seedlings when the first pair of real leaves appeared above the seed leaves, or to earth up my potatoes when the stems reached a certain height, it brought me up short.

Like all the domestic skills I take for granted, it was my mother who showed me what to do in the garden, just as she taught me how to cast off a piece of knitting neatly, and lay royal icing over marzipan on a cake. None of which I think of as 'knowledge'.

To me, knowledge is learning how to conjugate a Latin verb, or bisect the angle of a triangle using a pair of compasses, or commit to memory the dates of the seventeenth-century Anglo-Dutch wars. I associate such 'knowledge' with formal education, school, university, and the things my father inculcated into me from as early as I can remember. One of my first conscious memories is of my father showing me how the pieces move on a chess-board. Another is an early birthday present of a set of mathematical instruments, each fitting neatly into its matching slot in a velvet-lined, midnight blue, leather case.

I do not think that this pure prejudice in favour of 'masculine' education was entirely of my own making. We were simply brought up to take a well-run home for granted. I remember my paternal grandmother – a formidable woman, with a razor-sharp intellect and an iron will – as permanently exasperated at the absence of any real role for her outside the domestic. She had been heavily involved in London local politics in the 1920s and 30s, but by the time I knew her, her intellectual energies were confined to the housekeeping, where she was only happy when performing a really difficult task with panache. I have a vivid mental picture of her with a smile of satisfaction on her face as she whipped two egg whites into stiff, brilliant white peaks to make meringues, on a flat dinner plate with an ordinary fork, the eggs held on the angled plate by the sheer force of her beating.

My generation took cookery and gardening for granted – just things our mothers had shown us how to do. I grew up in a world where the selection of fresh fruit and vegetables in shops or on market stalls closely matched what could be grown in any allotment. So I could easily emulate my mother's dishes, without even thinking.

Today, the fruit and vegetables sections of supermarkets are piled high with unfamiliar produce from every time zone and season. The recipes I learned without noticing are almost irrelevant to an adventurous young cook who wants to prepare 'exotic' dishes involving soy beans, or lemon grass, or callalou. Perhaps that is why TV celebrity chefs – demonstrating the latest fashionable dishes from the global kitchen – are so extraordinarily popular.

The tomato and potato were once strange foodstuffs, offering opportunities for an inventive new cuisine. Like them, all the exotic vegetables I just named will happily grow here in Britain. So now that I have conceded that gardening is something that requires to be learned, I am going to expand my horticultural horizons – resist my urge to succumb to the nostalgia of what I already know. Next season I'm planting chillies, okra and pak choi in my multi-coloured pots among the chimneys.